T0288585

National Defense Research Institute

Strategic and Performance Planning
for the Office of the Chancellor for Education and Professional Development in the Department of Defense

Dina G. Levy ✦ *Roger Benjamin* ✦ *Tora Kay Bikson*
Eric Derghazarian ✦ *James A. Dewar*
Susan M. Gates ✦ *Tessa Kaganoff* ✦ *Joy S. Moini*
Thomas S. Szayna ✦ *Ron W. Zimmer*

RAND

Prepared for the
Office of the Secretary of Defense

The research described in this report was sponsored by the Office of the Secretary of Defense (OSD). The research was conducted in RAND's National Defense Research Institute, a federally funded research and development center supported by the OSD, the Joint Staff, the unified commands, and the defense agencies under Contract DASW01-01-C-0004.

Library of Congress Cataloging-in-Publication Data

Strategic and performance planning for the Office of the Chancellor for Education and
  Professional Development in the Department of Defense / Dina G. Levy ... [et al.].
      p. cm.
    "MR-1234."
    Includes bibliographical references.
    ISBN 0-8330-3037-X
    1. United States. Office of the Chancellor for Education and Professional
  Development. 2. United States—Armed Forces—Civilian employees—Training of.
  3. Military education—United States. I. Levy, Dina G.

  UB153 .S77 2001
  355.6'1969—dc21

                                                                  2001048138

RAND is a nonprofit institution that helps improve policy and decisionmaking through research and analysis. RAND® is a registered trademark. RAND's publications do not necessarily reflect the opinions or policies of its research sponsors.

Published 2001 by RAND
1700 Main Street, P.O. Box 2138, Santa Monica, CA 90407-2138
1200 South Hayes Street, Arlington, VA 22202-5050
201 North Craig Street, Suite 102, Pittsburgh, PA 15213
RAND URL: http://www.rand.org/
To order RAND documents or to obtain additional information,
contact Distribution Services: Telephone: (310) 451-7002;
Fax: (310) 451-6915; Email: order@rand.org

A high-quality civilian workforce is an important element of a high-quality defense infrastructure. In an era of streamlining, demographic change, low unemployment, and rapid technological change, education, training, and development (ET&D) play a key role in maintaining and improving the quality of the workforce. In this environment, it is important for the Department of Defense (DoD) to ensure that the civilian workforce receives appropriate, high-quality ET&D in a cost-effective manner.

In October 1998, the DoD Office of the Chancellor for Education and Professional Development was established with the mission of being the principal advocate for the academic quality and cost-effectiveness of all DoD institutions, programs, and courses of instruction that provide education or professional development for DoD civilians. To carry out this mission, the office needs to develop a strategic and performance planning process.

At the request of the Chancellor's office, RAND has undertaken a study to examine several approaches to establishing visions, strategic plans, and implementation plans in a variety of ET&D contexts and to identify the aspects of each approach that might be most relevant and useful to the Chancellor's office in its strategic planning effort. The purpose of this report is to inform the Chancellor's office of the results of our research and to provide information that might be immediately helpful in building a strategic and performance planning process for the Chancellor's office.

Because the role of the Chancellor's office continues to evolve, and because strategic plans cannot be transplanted in their entirety from one organization to another, findings are presented as insights to be considered during the strategic planning process rather than as alternative complete strategic plans or strong recommendations for future courses of action. It should also be noted that some of the insights will be more or less viable depending on the political context at the time of consideration.

This research was conducted for the DoD Office of the Chancellor for Education and Professional Development within the Forces and Resources Policy Center of RAND's National Defense Research Institute, a federally funded research and development center sponsored by the Office of the Secretary of Defense, the Joint Staff, the Unified Commands, and the defense agencies.

CONTENTS

FIGURES

TABLES

With a civilian workforce of about 700,000, the Department of Defense (DoD) is one of the largest employers of civilians in the nation. Maintaining the quality of that workforce is one of its highest priorities. In October 1998, DoD established the Office of the Chancellor for Education and Professional Development to serve as the principal advocate for academic quality and cost-effectiveness of all institutions, programs, and courses of instruction that serve DoD civilian workers. The office, which exists and operates within the organizational hierarchy of the Office of the Secretary of Defense (OSD), is part of a complex network of organizations that set policy for education, training, and development (ET&D), manage the DoD civilian workforce, and provide ET&D services to DoD civilians. One of the first tasks of the new Chancellor and his staff is to determine how they can best influence academic quality and cost-effectiveness in such a complex environment.

STUDY OBJECTIVE AND APPROACH

This research is intended to help in that effort by conducting case studies of strategic planning in comparable institutions with reputations for high performance. The research team first reviewed the literature on strategic planning and designed an interview protocol used to gather information about strategic planning in interviews with institutional leaders. Then the team examined DoD civilian ET&D and the position of the Chancellor's office within the DoD ET&D system to identify key challenges and constraints the Chancellor's office faces in carrying out its mission. The team then conducted case studies of comparable institutions that are considered by their peers to be models of best practices in strategic planning. For ten institutions, the research team studied published vision statements, mission statements, strategic plans, and relevant implementation plans. For three others, the team also conducted site visits during which we interviewed institutional leaders involved in the strategic planning for education and professional development in their organizations.

This report includes in its appendices descriptions of the strategic planning process of each of these institutions. The body of the report describes a framework for analyzing strategic planning, key trends affecting DoD civilian ET&D, key challenges facing the Chancellor's office, and lessons from the case studies that appear most relevant to the Chancellor's office.

A FRAMEWORK FOR ANALYZING STRATEGIC PLANNING

We analyzed strategic planning by looking at four products of an organization's planning process: *mission, vision, strategy,* and *strategic plan*—in that order. The ordering is significant in that each succeeding product should be compatible with those that precede it. Not all planning processes result in these products, but we elected to include all four to provide the broadest framework for understanding how organizations similar to the Chancellor's office do strategic planning.

We defined these products in specific ways, as follows:

Mission. The mission sets out the obligations and commitments of the organization. The DoD Office of the Chancellor for Education and Professional Development's mission is stated in DoD Directive 5124.7: "to serve as the principal advocate for the academic quality and cost-effectiveness of all DoD civilian education and professional development activities."

Vision. Vision is an organization's unique sense of identity and shared sense of purpose. Although the Chancellor's office deferred the development of a vision until the completion of this study, it has at least three ways that it could envision its role:

1. *Director:* prescribing courses of action for the institutions;

2. *Expert:* acting as the information clearinghouse and the expert on quality and productivity; or

3. *Facilitator:* facilitating communications, spreading ideas, and supporting quality improvement.

Strategy. Strategy relates means to ends. This is a common, but not universal, definition of strategy.

Strategic Plan. A strategic plan is the set of actionable items to carry out the strategy. It turns the concept of strategy into actions. The plan identifies actions to handle specific challenges or constraints of the organization.

Our framework also took into consideration challenges that organizations face after they have developed a strategic plan—governance, implementation, monitoring, performance evaluation, adjustment, etc. In our interview protocol, we particularly asked questions about governance, implementation, and evaluation of performance, all of which are important for the Chancellor's office to understand during its formative stage.

TRENDS AFFECTING DoD CIVILIAN EDUCATION, TRAINING, AND DEVELOPMENT

The Future Military Operating Environment

The strategic plan for the U.S. armed forces over the next two decades provides the best projections we have of the evolution of the armed forces and the civilian workforce needed to support them. *Joint Vision 2020*, released by the Chairman of the Joint Chiefs of Staff in 2000, and its predecessor volume, *Joint Vision 2010*, forecast a fighting force that is more technology-intensive, leaner, and more efficient in conducting operations that are characterized by greater precision, timeliness, and full access to information. The civilian workforce supporting such a fighting force will need to be proficient in using information technology, problem solving, communications skills, and the ability to work within and across complex organizations. The growing need for such high-level skills will elevate the importance of education, training, and development.

Demographic Trends in the DoD Civilian Workforce

The two demographic characteristics of most importance to educating the civilian workforce are education level and age distribution. The average level of education in the civilian force has been increasing slightly, but most future recruits are expected to have only a high school diploma, as has been true in the past.[1] Because the workforce will increasingly need more advanced skills, education, training, and development programs will likely bear some of the responsibility for teaching those skills.[2]

The civilian workforce is also aging. Over 80 percent of the current force is over age 40 and one-third is age 51 or older. This has two important implications for civilian workforce education: (1) because there will be a massive turnover in personnel as older workers retire (about 230,000 civilian personnel are expected to retire in the next 14 years), education, training, and development programs need to target new recruits, and (2) other programs will need to continue to serve more mature workers who will be in the workforce over the next 10 to 20 years. If the U.S. economy remains strong over this period, the DoD will face increasing competition from the private sector in hiring skilled workers. If the DoD finds that it needs to recruit less-skilled workers as a result of competition, this trend will put even greater demands on DoD civilian ET&D.

Federal Laws that Promote Strategic Planning and Outcomes-Based Assessment

In the 1990s, Congress passed several laws that address waste and inefficiency in federal agencies. Potentially the most important of these for the Chancellor's office is the Government Performance and Results Act (GPRA) of 1993, which directs the largest federal agencies to submit five-year strategic plans and annual performance plans along with their budget requests to Congress. Success in carrying out

---

[1]Defense Manpower Data Center: https://www.dmdc.osd.mil/ids/owa/ids (general website); https://www.dmdc.osd.mil/ids/owa/ids_Rpts#CIV (password protected website).

[2]Note, however, that the Office of the Deputy Assistant Secretary of Defense for Civilian Personnel Policy suspects that educational data are underreported for employees who complete education after initial hiring.

the requirements of the GPRA has been mixed as agencies undertake the difficult task of changing agency operations and processes to create a more performance-based and results-oriented culture. In fiscal year 2001, most agency strategic and performance plans are still considered to be of dubious quality, and the General Accounting Office and the Congress are continuing to work with them in making the needed improvements. Nonetheless, such a movement is creating an atmosphere that supports the efforts of the Chancellor's office to ensure quality and cost-effectiveness in DoD civilian ET&D.

Quality Assurance Movement in Higher Education

Increasing demands for greater accountability for public spending are leading higher education institutions to develop ways to demonstrate both their effectiveness and their efforts at improvement. The responses to the demands for accountability have taken a variety of forms (e.g., the development of new types of student assessment, experimentation with new forms of accreditation, and adoption of practices from the business world). The Chancellor's office will benefit from the pioneering efforts of many of these institutions to both measure quality and increase cost-effectiveness.

CHALLENGES IN DoD CIVILIAN EDUCATION AND WORKFORCE PLANNING

Characteristics of DoD Civilian Education, Training, and Development

Many stakeholder groups are involved in DoD civilian ET&D, including provider organizations (i.e., those offering education services), customer organizations (e.g., the DoD functional sponsors of the institutions), the consumer population (i.e., the entire DoD civilian workforce), and the Office of the Chancellor. Each stakeholder brings its own set of challenges to the task of quality assurance.

The OSD sponsors more than 20 institutions and numerous programs and independent courses of instruction serving DoD civilians. Countless other courses and programs for DoD civilian personnel are available through institutions run by the Army, Navy, Air Force, and Marine Corps, as well as through non-DoD providers. The wide variety of programs spread across many institutions of different types vastly complicates the formation of any uniform set of criteria for evaluating quality and cost-effectiveness.

There are also many customers of DoD civilian ET&D in addition to the functional sponsors of the institutions. These include the Joint Chiefs of Staff and the OSD principal staff assistants, as well as Congress, and the commanders and directors of the provider institutions. As for the student population, its sheer size and geographic dispersion present problems of management, tracking, and delivery of services. The age structure of the civilian workforce also poses difficulties, since many workers have reached the highest level they can attain in their career field and have less incentive to pursue professional development.

The Chancellor's office was designed to serve as an intermediary organization between these various stakeholders. As such, it has limited authority over institutions, programs, and courses of instruction. Its key challenge may be how to effect change in a complex system within which it has little authority.

Challenges for the Chancellor's Office and the DoD Workforce Planning System

ET&D is just one element of a much larger workforce planning strategy. Currently, the DoD and the Chancellor's office do not have a conceptual framework that articulates the DoD's overarching educational needs or that helps persuade sponsors to adequately resource needed changes. Moreover, the Chancellor's office has been charged with promoting academic quality and cost-effectiveness but has been afforded only limited authority over funds, institutions, programs, and courses of instruction. Thus, there are two categories of challenges facing DoD civilian ET&D: those facing the civilian workforce planning system in using ET&D as a tool to improve the workforce and those facing the Chancellor's office as it develops a strategy to assess the quality and cost-effectiveness of education, training, and development.

THE CASE STUDIES AND LESSONS LEARNED

With these characteristics and challenges in mind, the research team identified seven organizational types whose responsibilities and challenges are comparable to the Chancellor's office:

- Accrediting agencies,
- Corporate universities and human resources departments,
- DoD professional military education, training, and development systems,
- Other federal agencies,
- Higher education systems and universities,
- Professional societies, labor unions, and
- State boards of higher education.

Within these types, we chose 13 organizations to serve as case studies on the basis of their reputations as best practice organizations among their peers. Two organizational types in the list shared the most characteristics with the Chancellor's office: state boards of higher education and other federal agencies. The research team visited three such organizations: the State Higher Education Planning Boards in Texas and Kentucky and the Department of Transportation (DoT), a government agency reputed to have a successful strategy for the education and professional development of its workers.

By examining the strategic planning efforts of these institutions, we identified strategies that the Chancellor's office could pursue, both within and outside its current charter. And for strategies within its charter, we further segregated our findings into three categories: near-term actions to be considered for the next two to three years, medium-term strategies for the next five years, and strategies that the Chancellor's office should employ over its lifetime.

Working Within the Charter of the Chancellor's Office

Near-Term Actions

- *Become the information center.* The Chancellor's office should consider developing a reputation as the primary source of quality information about education in the DoD. This strategy has been very successful in similar organizations.

- *Include stakeholders in strategy development.* The most prevalent strategy for making decisions that affect multiple stakeholders is to include them in the decisionmaking process. Many of the institutions studied have effectively used this strategy.

- *Define specific strategies for stakeholder groups.* Different stakeholders will have different needs and priorities. By acknowledging those differences, the Chancellor's office can enhance the effectiveness of the strategic plan.

- *Differentiate among multiple missions.* Any initial mission differentiation distinctions the Chancellor's office makes will, in turn, shape subsequent relationships and decisions of the Chancellor's office. A good example of this can be found in the formulation of the California Master Plan.

- *Develop assessment criteria.* The Chancellor's office needs to identify and reach agreement on assessment criteria, standards, and benchmarks for all relevant institutions offering education, training, and development.

Medium-Term Strategies

- *Gain agreement for specific reporting requirements.* The Chancellor's office needs to formalize some basic reporting requirements that will help it function. Reporting arrangements themselves appear to have significant effects on the behavior of institutions.

- *Acquire a role in the program approval process.* The Texas Higher Education Coordinating Board has the authority to approve or disapprove programs eligible for state funding and can recommend changes to the higher education funding formula and raise other issues to the legislature. Such authority gives stature and influence to the organization.

- *Eliminate governance obstacles.* As the Chancellor's office develops its programs, existing lines of authority may prove to be too complex or unclear. Under these circumstances, the Chancellor's office may wish to make recommendations to remedy the situation.

Lifetime Strategies

- *Play a flexible role.* Organizations in the business of assessing the quality and productivity of postsecondary education always face a changing set of external pressures, particularly vacillations in budgets. As a result, intermediary organizations must help providers adopt a flexible approach to respond to these changes.

- *Use different strategies for different institutions.* Rather than trying to develop a single definition of quality, it may be more effective to focus on different definitions depending on the type of institution or program evaluated. The case studies demonstrate how several organizations have implemented such an approach.

- *Establish a constituency for reforms.* Several case studies demonstrate the effectiveness of playing a participatory role—rather than a commanding role—in quality assurance. This is accomplished by involving all stakeholders in improving standards, by providing information about standards and performance, and by offering examples of model practice.

Strategies Currently Outside the Charter of the Chancellor's Office

Identify salient obstacles and incentives for members of the workforce. The Chancellor's office should consider analyzing the key factors underlying the inadequacy of civilian participation in education and professional development and launching outreach activities to address these factors.

Promote the strategic role of education, training, and development. An effective strategy for the Department of Transportation has been its emphasis on the connection between learning and organizational performance. Its campaign stresses that learning is an investment and not an expense.

Engage sponsors in the education, training, and development effort.
Our case studies provide several examples of strategies used to encourage line managers to promote professional development among
their workers.

Promote a demand-driven system. Currently, DoD ET&D for civilians
is supply-driven, with programs offered without much regard for the
demands of the workforce or customer organizations. It should take
cues from the DoT, which—by encouraging managers to develop
professional development activities based on workforce needs—is
working to create a demand-driven system.

Use education to compensate for recruiting difficulties. Faced with an
aging DoD workforce and with competition from the private sector
for new hires, the Chancellor's office needs to support lifetime employee learning and development programs. This will both cultivate
the Defense Department's existing workforce and help offset its reduced success in recruiting new personnel.

NEXT STEPS

The Chancellor's office faces a truly unique set of challenges and opportunities. No organization we studied parallels the situation of the
Chancellor's office well enough to recommend adoption of that organization's course of action or planning process. In the light of such
a situation, the literature suggests the instinct in the Chancellor's office to develop a clear sense of identity/purpose is a good one. By
our definition, this is the development of a clear vision. That should
be the next strategic step for the Chancellor's office.

Having codified a clear sense of identity/purpose, the next step
should be the development of a strategy for accomplishing the purpose that includes, first, a governance structure, and that is mindful
of the lessons identified in this study. A variety of strategy development techniques exist for this purpose, and a number of organizations are available for assistance in this arena. RAND will aid the
Chancellor's office in drawing upon these resources in its future efforts.

We thank Susan Hosek for the guidance she provided as director of the program under which this report was produced. We also bene-fited from discussions with James Hosek, Robert Schoeni, and Susan Everingham before the preparation of this report. Albert Robbert and Patricia Gumport provided reviews of an earlier draft, greatly enhancing the quality of the report, and Catherine Augustine, Laura Zakaras, and Gordon Lee helped refine its structure and content. Lisa Hochman and Shirley Cromb provided helpful secretarial sup-port.

We greatly appreciate the cooperation of all participants in the in-terviews at our case study sites. They afforded us the opportunity to learn about aspects of the strategic planning processes in their orga-nizations that were not documented in any literature.

Chancellor Jerome Smith, James Raney, John Dill, Beverly Popelka, Leslye McDade-Morrison, and Donna Brown of the DoD Office of the Chancellor for Education and Professional Development supported our efforts and provided useful feedback on the research leading up to this report.

AMA	American Medical Association
AR	Army Regulation
ARPRINT	Army's Program for Individual Training
ASA	Assistant Secretary of the Army
ASD (FMP)	Assistant Secretary of Defense for Force Management Policy
CB	Coordinating Board
CCC	California Community Colleges
CFO	Chief Financial Officer
CHE	Council of Higher Education
CJCS	Chairman of the Joint Chiefs of Staff
CPE	Council for Postsecondary Education
CPEC	California Postsecondary Education Commission
CSU	California State University
DASD (CPP)	Deputy Assistant Secretary of Defense for Civilian Personnel Policy
DCSOPS	Deputy Chief of Staff for Operations

DCSPER   Deputy Chief of Staff for Personnel

DLIFLC   Defense Language Institute Foreign Language Center

DoD   Department of Defense

DoT   Department of Transportation

ET&D   Education, Training, and Development

FHWA   Federal Highway Administration

FIRSCo   Fidelity Institutional Retirement Services Company

FM   Field Manual

GAO   General Accounting Office

GPRA   Government Performance and Results Act

HB1   House Bill 1

ITS   Intelligent Transportation System

L&D   Learning and Development

LDC   Learning and Development Council

MDEP   Management Decision Packages

MOS   Military Occupational Speciality

MRA   Manpower and Reserve Affairs

MRC   Major Regional Contingency

NCO   Noncommissioned Officer

OA   Operating Administration

OMB   Office of Management and Budget

OSD   Office of the Secretary of Defense

OST   Office of the Secretary of Transportation

OUSD   Office of the Under Secretary of Defense

PCB   Professional Capacity Building

PEG   Program Evaluation Group

PERSCOM   Personnel Command

PPBES   Planning, Programming, Budgeting and Execution System

PPBS   Planning, Programming, and Budgeting System

QAA   Quality Assurance Agency

QDR   Quadrennial Defense Review

RSIC   Redstone Scientific Information Center

SACS   Southern Association of Colleges and Schools

SCOPE   Strategic Committee on Postsecondary Education

SDU   Service Delivery University

SMDR   Structure Manning Decision Review

SSA   Social Security Administration

TRADOC   Training and Doctrine Command

UC   University of California

UK   University of Kentucky

USD (P&R)   Under Secretary of Defense for Personnel and Readiness

WASC   Western Association of Schools and Colleges

Chapter One

INTRODUCTION

BACKGROUND

With a civilian workforce of about 700,000, the Department of Defense (DoD) is one of the largest employers within the federal government and one of the largest employers in our nation more generally. In the current era of streamlining, demographic change, low unemployment, and rapid technological change, employers face a tremendous challenge in developing and maintaining a workforce with the skills required for a high level of performance.

The DoD, like many other public and private sector employers, offers its civilian workforce opportunities for education, training, and development in institutions, programs, and courses of instruction run by both the department and externally. In FY 1997, the Office of the Secretary of Defense (OSD) sponsored 20 institutions and 36 autonomous programs serving DoD civilians. In addition, 68 programs serving the needs of civilian personnel were offered by more than 40 external providers.

The DoD study report, *Management Reform Memorandum 3: Streamlining the Management of Educational and Professional Development Programs,* was published by the Office of the Assistant Secretary of Defense for Force Management Policy (ASD (FMP)) in December 1997.[1] The Defense Reform Initiative Directive 41 study report, *Blueprint for the Chancellor for Education and Professional*

---

[1]This report describes the programs offered in detail.

1

Development, was issued in September 1998 (Cohen, 1998). These studies provided background, rationale, and recommendations for establishing the DoD Office of the Chancellor for Education and Professional Development. In October 1998, the Chancellor's office was established with the mission of being the principal advocate for the academic quality and cost-effectiveness of all DoD institutions, programs, and courses of instruction that provide education or professional development for DoD civilians. To carry out this mission, the office needs to develop a strategic and performance planning process.

RESEARCH OBJECTIVE

The overall objective of this project is to support the Office of the Chancellor for Education and Professional Development in formulating and establishing a strategic and performance planning process. In this endeavor, the Chancellor's office faces both the problem and the advantage of starting from scratch, as no position akin to that of the Chancellor existed in the DoD before 1998. Because of its recent establishment, the office has limited information at its fingertips, and important realms of responsibility remain unclear. The advantage of this situation, however, is that the new office can define its vision and outline its strategic plan relatively unencumbered by past planning procedures, goals, and objectives.

APPROACH

To inform the development of a strategic and performance planning process based on the best practices currently available, we have focused the research along four main lines.

We began by surveying the literature on strategic planning in higher education, business, and government to develop a standard framework within which to study the strategic planning efforts of organizations similar to the Chancellor's office. One result of this effort was the development of the interview protocol we used to gather information about strategic planning in other organizations. The protocol is provided in Appendix A.

Next, we set out to characterize the most important dimensions of the Chancellor's office and its environment. We looked at both trends affecting the role of the Chancellor's office and key challenges or constraints it faces. This exercise enabled us to systematically identify classes of organizations that could be considered most similar to the Chancellor's office in terms of key aspects of their structure or situation and thus perhaps yield the most in terms of relevant insights into the strategic planning process.

A third component of the research effort was to identify specific institutions from each class considered most similar to the Chancellor's office and to collect detailed information on their strategic planning efforts, from the development of a vision to the maintenance of an implementation plan. Here, we selected institutions with a reputation for having developed successful strategic plans. We studied ten examples spanning eight types of organizations using published vision statements, mission statements, strategic plans, and relevant implementation plans. Appendix B summarizes the strategic planning efforts of those institutions.

We also conducted in-depth case studies of two state higher education planning boards—those in Kentucky and Texas—as well as a government agency that is reputed to have a successful strategy for offering professional development opportunities to its employees— the Department of Transportation (along with the Federal Highway Administration). In each case, we visited the site and conducted in-depth interviews with top administrators involved in strategic planning for education and professional development in their organizations. The information gathered during those interviews is presented in Appendix C.

Finally, we synthesized findings from our studies and extracted relevant insights for the Chancellor's office. In some cases, we highlight characteristics that the office may wish to emulate, and in other cases, we warn against pitfalls the Chancellor's office should seek to avoid. We ended our effort with a look at potential next steps for the Chancellor's office.

ORGANIZATION OF THE REPORT

Our conceptual framework for strategic planning is outlined in Chapter Two. Chapter Three presents a picture of current trends affecting DoD civilian education, training, and development (ET&D) and the role of the Chancellor's office in the DoD ET&D system. In Chapter Four, we characterize current features of civilian ET&D and identify key challenges and constraints faced by the Chancellor's office. We also discuss related workforce planning challenges. Chapter Five uses the challenges identified in Chapter Four as a foundation for assessing similarity between the Chancellor's office and other organizations. It ends with a list of specific sites selected for case study. Finally, in Chapter Six, we highlight key insights uncovered in the case studies and suggest next steps for the Chancellor's office in the development of a strategic and performance planning process.

Three appendices contain details of the case study process and findings not included in the body of the report. Appendix A presents the protocol that was used to structure interviews conducted during our site visits and that also served as a guide when gathering and presenting information from literature-based case studies. Appendix B contains detailed case studies from the literature and Appendix C contains extensive notes from the site visits.

Chapter Two

A FRAMEWORK FOR STRATEGIC PLANNING ANALYSIS

In colloquial terms, the mission of the Chancellor's office (within the constraints of its charter) is to help enhance DoD ET&D to create and maintain a "world class support force." Part of the impetus for the creation of the Chancellor's office was that there was not a well-defined strategic perspective for ensuring the quality and productivity of DoD civilian postsecondary education. The adoption of a strategic perspective could improve the ability of the Chancellor's office and others to serve the educational needs of the DoD civilian population. Accordingly, the Chancellor's office asked RAND to examine the strategic planning approaches used by organizations in situations similar to those it faces.

Because no situation is exactly like that of the Chancellor's office, and because many types of similarities were potentially of interest, we looked at a wide variety of educational cases ranging from classical and corporate universities to accrediting agencies to state boards of higher education. This, in turn, caused us to think more broadly about terms such as "workforce" and even "strategic planning."

The strategic planning literature focuses primarily on planning approaches used in for-profit organizations in the private sector. Although the strategic planning challenges of the DoD and of educational institutions share many characteristics with the for-profit organizations, both have important differences as well. The DoD, for example, is more interested in risk-averse strategic planning whereas the private sector has a much greater tolerance for the failure of strategic plans.[1] However, even if their challenges were identical to those of the private sector, they would still share the private sector's confusion of terms such as "strategic" (as opposed to long-range), "planning" (as opposed to programming or budgeting), and "strategic planning" (as opposed to strategic thinking or visioning).

The private sector planning literature today is dominated by treatises on planning in uncertain times,[2] with particular emphasis on planning in the face of e-commerce opportunities.[3] Although the Chancellor's office faces some uncertainty related to its workforce situation and the effect of the Internet on that workforce, little in the current literature is applicable to the situation of the Chancellor's office. More appropriate for its situation is the traditional work on the purposes and processes of strategic planning. Much of RAND's work on strategic planning[4] and visions[5] is aligned with traditional models. In our discussion of various approaches to planning, we will adopt definitions for several terms related to strategic planning and then translate others' uses of these terms into our terms. This approach carries with it all the attendant dangers of translation in general, but it should bring the terms surrounding strategic planning into a reasonably common framework. We were particularly careful in the interview protocol to ask what definitions people were using for the major strategic planning terms.

Just as there is a variety of definitions for many of the terms involved in strategic planning, there are many descriptions of strategic planning as a process. For the purposes of this report, we will choose one, define the terms involved in it, and then to the extent possible,

---

[1]For instance, consider DoD planning for two simultaneous major regional contingencies (MRCs) and then two near-simultaneous MRCs in the *Bottom-Up Review* during a time when the U.S. public was hard pressed to accept the potential for even a single MRC. Contrast that with a "dot com" that will set a strategic plan on little more than an idea and youthful enthusiasm, or contrast it with industry giant Microsoft taking a very risky plunge in changing its strategy 90 degrees toward the Internet.

[2]See, for example, *Harvard Business Review on Managing Uncertainty*, Harvard Business School Press (1999); Mintzberg (1994); Hamel and Prahalad (1994); and Porter (1998).

[3]Popular recent works include Evans and Wurster (1999); Locke (2000); Christensen (1997); and Modahl (1999).

[4]See, for example, Dewar et al. (1993).

[5]See, for example, Setear et al. (1990).

translate descriptions of the strategic planning processes of other organizations.

In investigating the strategic planning process of an organization, the products rather than the process itself are often observed. In rare cases, the process by which the products were achieved is also reported. Nonetheless, the products of an organization's planning process are indicative of some aspects of the process and form a starting point for the research. In addition to looking for any information specifically on an organization's planning process, we looked for four products: *mission, vision, strategy,* and *strategic plan*—in that order. The ordering is significant in that each succeeding product should be compatible with those that precede it. Not all planning processes result in these four products, but we elected to include all four to provide the broadest framework for understanding how organizations similar to the Chancellor's office do strategic planning.

In our terms, the mission sets out the obligations and commitments of the organization. Some organizations (typically subordinate organizations such as the Chancellor's office) have obligations and commitments given to them when they are created. Other organizations (such as some universities and businesses) develop commitments or obligations as part of a planning effort. Still others (more typically businesses) have implicit obligations and commitments (e.g., to shareholders, customers).

The DoD Office of the Chancellor for Education and Professional Development's mission is stated in DoD Directive 5124.7: "to serve as the principal advocate for the academic quality and cost-effectiveness of all DoD civilian education and professional development activities."

By vision, we mean an organization's unique sense of identity and shared sense of purpose. This is consistent with the work on successful visionary companies by Collins and Porras, work on high-performing organizations by Vaill, as well as work RAND has done on the attributes of a good vision.[6] It is a relatively uncommon definition of vision, but then, vision is rarely defined. Most often, visions are construed as goals, and vision statements are "feel good" exhor-

----

[6]See Collins and Porras (1994); Vaill (1982), pp. 23–39; and Setear et al. (1990).

tations about the lofty aims of an organization.[7] On the other hand, our definition of vision is in keeping with some of the ideas of the Chancellor's office on vision. Although the Chancellor's office has deferred the development of a vision until the results of this study are reported, it does have some candidates for identity/purpose. Among them are

- *Director*:   prescribing courses of action for the institutions,

- *Expert*: acting as the information clearinghouse and the expert on quality and productivity, and

- *Facilitator*: facilitating communications, spreading ideas, and encouraging and supporting the process of quality improvement.

Before proceeding, it is important to note that there is a serious confusion in practice between mission and vision. In some sectors, such as the military, mission definitely comes first (as it has in the case of the Chancellor's office). In other sectors, mission follows from vision and in yet others, mission and vision are used interchangeably. In the protocol developed for the site visits, the first series of questions was aimed at understanding how that organization used terms such as mission, vision, and strategy to make the translation into the framework above.

Strategy relates means to ends. This is a common (but not universal) definition of strategy. In Mintzberg's (1994) work, strategy formulation is a creative exercise with a clear problem to solve: It is the translation of the vision into a clear *concept* of what will work within the current and future environment and within resource constraints.

The strategic plan is the set of actionable items to carry out the strategy. It turns the concept of strategy into actions. Mintzberg calls this "strategic programming" because it is the more mechanistic implementation of the creative insight embodied in the strategy. The plan identifies actions to handle specific challenges or constraints of the organization.

---

[7]Simpson (1998) gives a good example: To wit, "We are committed to an organisational capability and mindset which guarantees rapidly delivering exceptional customer and stakeholder value by negotiating and making the appropriate trade-offs among schedule, quality, cost, functionality, technology limits and resources."

After the plan is developed, there are still important questions of governance, implementation, monitoring, performance evaluation, adjustment, etc. In our interview protocol, we asked questions particularly about governance, implementation, and evaluation of performance. The governance structures that enable or complicate implementation actions are particularly important elements for the Chancellor's office to understand as it formalizes its governance structure.

Governance involves the decisionmaking units, policies, or procedures, written or unwritten, that influence resource allocation. Therefore, in examining any institution it is important to understand the formal governance arrangements that flow down from the board of trustees or other repositories of formal governance powers. However, it is equally important to ascertain how narrow or wide the ability to influence resource allocation decisions is in an institution. For our purposes, influence may be viewed as forming a continuum from persuasion or advocacy to control over whether b will follow the wishes of a in a particular decision.

It is useful to think of governance in three ways: Two focus on governance issues internal to the institution and the third focuses on external governance issues. First, there is the question of the characterization of the basic governance system of the unit being examined. Does the entity have formal powers of control over the agencies under its purview, or is it more accurate to speak of facilitative, coordinative, or advocacy roles being primary? Second, scope and complexity in number and lines of authority, responsibility, and accountability must be considered. The programs or institutions falling under the aegis of the unit of governance in question can be measured in terms of these concepts. Third, these same governance concepts, then, can be used to analyze the relationships between the institution itself and the external institutions to which it reports or relates in some fashion.

The governance system put in place should ideally flow out of the mission statement of the institution. The development of the implementation strategy will be guided by the nature of the governance system in place. For example, if the governance system in question has basic authority to compel units under its purview to implement its actions, this will suggest one sort of implementation strategy, command in orientation. However, if the governance unit has only powers of persuasion, then another implementation strategy might be suggested, perhaps one based on providing useful information.

The evaluation of performance is a check on how the organization could tell if the plan it developed was performing as desired. This is an important connection between what was intended and what happened. That is, it is important to know that being a high-performance organization was the result of intentional actions rather than simply luck or some other set of circumstances.

Our interview protocol (Appendix A) included questions aimed at the strategic planning products and processes discussed above. It also included general questions about the assessment of quality and cost-effectiveness to collect more detail on implementation and to support RAND's other research for the Chancellor's office on quality and productivity evaluation.[8]

----

[8]See Gates et al. (2001).

Chapter Three

TRENDS AFFECTING DoD CIVILIAN EDUCATION, TRAINING, AND DEVELOPMENT

Devising a plan aimed at helping to ensure the quality and cost-effectiveness of DoD civilian ET&D should start with the overall mission of the DoD and the role of the civilians in it. DoD civilians play an integral role making the U.S. armed forces well-trained, well-equipped, and well-led and thus contribute to deterring threats to U.S. interests and ensuring the security of the United States. In this sense, the overall plans of development of the U.S. armed forces also provide the basic frame of reference for the future DoD civilian workforce. Within these constraints, the demographic characteristics of the current DoD civilian workforce clarify further the likely needs in the realm of ET&D for civilians supporting the warfighter. We see these two factors—the overall direction of development of the DoD (along with the resulting changes in the roles of civilians) and the demographic characteristics of the current DoD civilian workforce—as the most important contextual considerations for the effort of the Chancellor's office to draw up a strategic plan to assure the quality and cost-effectiveness of DoD civilian ET&D.

Complicating the task, the Chancellor's office forms but one of the multiple stakeholders involved in the education, training, and development of the DoD civilian workforce. The Chancellor's office serves as one interface between the DoD civilian workforce, entities external to the DoD (e.g., Congress), and the education community at large. Changes occurring in several domains, therefore, can affect the outcome of the office's efforts. Moreover, the Chancellor's office must take into account the unique characteristics and concerns of the other stakeholders.

Although the task of the Chancellor's office has many pitfalls, recent legislation that aims to improve accountability and effectiveness of the federal agencies, as evidenced by the Government Performance and Results Act (GPRA) of 1993, amounts to pressure toward a more results-oriented approach within the DoD and provides support to the strategic planning effort of the Chancellor's office. In addition, evolving trends in the higher education community toward ensuring quality and productivity in education may have application in the professional development of the federal workforce in general and, more specifically, of the DoD civilian workforce. The Chancellor's office can learn from and apply some of these methods as it puts together a plan suited specifically to the current and future needs of the DoD civilian workforce.

In this chapter, we first highlight the overall strategic direction of the DoD to provide an overview of the projected operating environment for the DoD civilian workforce. Next, we highlight some of the most important demographic characteristics of the current DoD civilian workforce and the future problems and constraints that these characteristics may pose in the realm of education, training, and development. Then, we touch briefly on the legislative efforts in favor of greater accountability in the work of federal agencies. Finally, we survey some of the innovations in the area of quality assurance in higher education from the perspective of providing the most useful lessons to the Chancellor's office.

THE FUTURE MILITARY OPERATING ENVIRONMENT

Joint Vision 2020 (JV 2020), released by the Chairman of the Joint Chiefs of Staff in May 2000, presents the strategic guidance for the evolution of the U.S. armed forces for the next two decades. The document, building on its predecessor, *Joint Vision 2010 (JV 2010)*, released in 1997, provides a common direction for services, combatant commands, defense agencies, and military-related businesses as they develop and transform to meet the security challenges facing the United States in the 21st century. *JV 2020* and *JV 2010*, as well as associated documents designed to provide more detailed guidelines to the services concerning development, training, and organization of the force,[1] provide the starting point for projections of the operating environment for the DoD civilian workforce.

The general aim of *JV 2020* remains the same as of *JV 2010*, namely, to use new technologies and information superiority to develop four new operational concepts (dominant maneuver, precision engagement, full-dimensional protection, and focused logistics) that will lead to full spectrum dominance for the U.S. armed forces. *JV 2020* stresses interoperability, innovation, and decision superiority as the central factors to the success of the four operational concepts.

The armed forces and the DoD in general have only begun to explore the operational and organizational implications of these changes and many of the consequences remain not yet fully understood. But regardless of these unknowns, the focus on innovation and use of information technology entails a reliance on high-quality people, who are adaptable and capable of innovative leadership. In an overall sense, the future force will be a more technology-intensive, leaner, and efficient organization, characterized by precision, timeliness, and full access to information. The civilian workforce will need to adjust accordingly in terms of skills, education, training, and development. Both *JV 2020* and *JV 2010* also place emphasis on jointness and unity of effort within the DoD to achieve the ambitious goal of a dramatic increase in military capabilities. Because the DoD civilian workforce forms an integral part of the department and civilians and uniformed staff work side by side and interact constantly, the appropriateness of education, training, and development of DoD civilians amounts to a crucial aspect in the ability of the U.S. armed forces to meet the goals outlined in *JV 2020* and *JV 2010*.

Besides the overall direction for the DoD suggested in *JV 2020* and *JV 2010*, the DoD civilian workforce is also being affected by the ongoing and complementary effort to integrate the best practices from the private sector into the way that the DoD functions. Spurred by the 1998 Defense Reform Initiative, the DoD has increased the use of business practices, such as consolidation of redundant functions,

---

[1]These documents include *Concept for Future Joint Operations* (1997), *21st Century Challenges and Desired Operational Capabilities* (1997), *Joint Vision Implementation Master Plan* (1998).

pursuing commercial alternatives where possible, and organizational streamlining. Recommendations along these lines have existed for years, but the downsizing of the DoD civilian workforce in the 1990s may have provided the needed push to implement such measures. For example, there has been increasing pressure to adhere to the Office of Management and Budget's (OMB's) policy of outsourcing whenever possible.[2] The greater acceptance of business practices also means that the technical, managerial, and leadership skills in demand in the private sector will become more important within the DoD civilian workforce.

From a perspective of a decade or more, the overall trends stemming from the move toward the armed forces envisioned in *JV 2020* and *JV 2010* as well as the widespread introduction of business practices into the DoD are likely to have a profound transformational effect on the DoD civilian workforce. The direction of this transformation is already foreshadowed in the changes in job distributions of DoD civilian workers that have come about in the latter half of the 1990s. Most of all, there has been a trend toward the relative growth of ad-ministrative and professional functions of the DoD civilian workforce in 1996–1999 (see Figure 3.1).

So far, these trends may have stemmed as much from downsizing choices as from the imperatives that led to the formulation of the two *Joint Vision* documents. But these trends are likely to deepen in the future. It will become increasingly important for the DoD workforce in general, and civilians in particular, to use information technology, improve problem-solving skills, and engage in continuous job-related skill development, all in a work environment that will require improved communication skills and the ability to work within and across complex organizations.[3] The changes in skill needs suggest commensurate changes in ET&D. The shifts depicted above are not unique. Indeed, they parallel the trends in the private sector. But the trends elevate the importance of the role that ET&D plays in main-taining and improving the quality of the DoD civilian workforce.

---

[2]OMB Circular No. A-76 suggests that "the Government should not compete with its citizens" (OMB, 1983, p. 1) and that the government should outsource those activities that are not inherently governmental.

[3]See Levy et al. (2001) for a characterization of work and workers needed for the future environment.

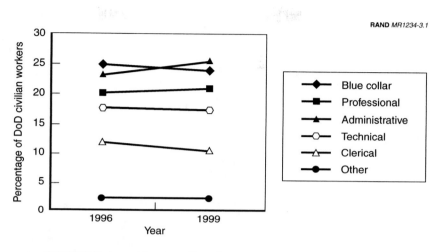

RAND *MR1234-3.1*

SOURCE: Defense Manpower Data Center (1999).

Figure 3.1—DoD Civilian Workforce, by Category of Occupation, 1996–1999

DEMOGRAPHIC TRENDS IN THE DoD CIVILIAN WORKFORCE

The two primary demographic characteristics particularly relevant to developing a strategy of educating and training the DoD civilian workforce are educational level and age distribution. The level of education in the DoD workforce has increased over the last decade (see Figure 3.2). In 1999, 31 percent of the workforce had an advanced degree (bachelor's degree or master's degree or more),[4] compared to 27 percent in 1989. Taking the attainment of an advanced degree as a proxy indicator of greater technical and problem-solving skills, the trend is consistent with the objectives outlined in *JV 2020* and *JV 2010*. We expect it to continue, although a major unknown is the ability of the DoD to attract similarly highly educated civilians to replace the DoD civilians who will retire in this decade.

---

[4]Note, however, that the Office of the Deputy Assistant Secretary of Defense for Civilian Personnel Policy (DASD (CPP)) suspects that educational data are underreported for employees who complete education after initial hiring.

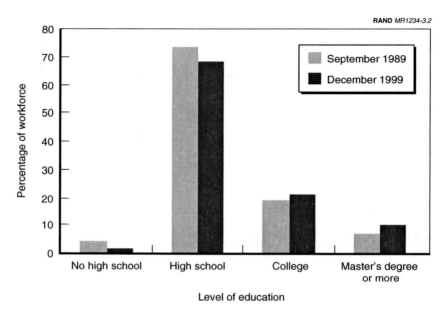

SOURCE: Defense Manpower Data Center (1999).

Figure 3.2—Educational Attainment Levels of the DoD Civilian Workforce, 1989–1999

There are a number of long-term implications for the Chancellor's office as a result of the trend toward greater educational attainment levels among the DoD civilian workforce. In the near-term, the trend may lead to a need to reevaluate ongoing ET&D programs, as a more educated workforce may need a different set of development opportunities. In a longer-term perspective, the Chancellor's office may face the opposite problem, if replacements for the DoD civilians who will retire in this decade are less-skilled and less-educated.

Although the demographic characteristics of the replacements of the retiring DoD civilians are in the realm of recruitment, and thus outside the Chancellor's immediate scope of responsibilities, they are important considerations for the office's strategic planning effort for several reasons. First, projections show that in 2000–06, an additional 17.6 million people will work in the service industry, which includes high-tech jobs, whereas the manufacturing industry is projected to lose 350,000 jobs.[5] The service sector clearly will be the primary magnet for entrants to the workforce, and the DoD will face increased competition for the kind of entrants it wishes to recruit. In turn, this will heighten the importance of including ET&D as part of the recruitment process.[6] Because of this, DoD workforce planners may wish to focus on ET&D opportunities not only to improve the skill levels of new and existing employees but also to serve as a part of the recruiting mechanism. Second, the DoD will have to compete with a larger labor market that is paying a premium to attract highly educated individuals possessing the skills that the DoD needs. The premium paid by the private sector, coupled with the rigid pay scale employed by the DoD (and the federal government as a whole) may make it increasingly difficult to attract and retain personnel with high-quality technical skills.[7] Third, in the period up to 2020, attracting college-educated personnel to the DoD may become more difficult if current changes in demographic patterns and in educational levels continue.[8] But in view of the skill needs for the DoD civilian

_____

[5]Most of the projected service jobs in 2006 are in the executive, administrative, and managerial, professional specialty, technical, marketing and sales, and administrative support categories. (See Department of Labor, 1999, PDF Version, Chapter 1, "The Workplace," and Chapter 7, "Implications of Workplace Change.")

[6]The DoD always faces stiff competition when it tries to hire high-quality people. The conventional wisdom is that a subset of the population will forgo higher wages available in the private sector for increased job security. The problem that the DoD faces is that (1) the promise of job security has been diminished in the downsizing era, and (2) job security might not be enough anymore. People expect to move around and want to make sure that they are developing skills in their current job so that they are still employable even if their job goes away. In addition, the downsizing has led to decreased opportunities for advancement in the DoD. DoD civilian employees also appear to be experiencing increased competition for promotion from retired military personnel as a result of a change of law on October 1, 1999, allowing military retirees to draw their full military retirement pay as well as receive their full civilian pay. Finally, the introduction of the Federal Employees Retirement System has made easier the movement between government service and the private sector, leading to an increase in competition for skilled employees between the government and the private sector.

[7]Gibbs found a significant difference between salaries of private sector and federal government engineers. He also found that new graduates with bachelor's degrees in 1992 were less likely to work for the federal government than new graduates with bachelor's degrees were in 1981.

[8]Department of Labor (1999), Chapter 1, "The Workplace," and Chapter 7, "Implications of Workplace Change."

workforce implicit in *JV 2020* and *JV 2010*, drawing upon less-educated personnel in the future represents an especially difficult problem for the Chancellor's office and may require additional adjustments in the DoD's ET&D programs.

In terms of age distribution, more than 80 percent of the current DoD civil service workforce is above age 40 and a third of the work-force (33.1 percent) is age 51 or over (see Figure 3.3). This means that, as the force envisioned in *JV 2020* and *JV 2010* comes into being, a large turnover of personnel, caused by retirement, is going to affect the DoD civilian workforce. Besides being a mature workforce, the DoD civilians also constitute an aging workforce (see Figure 3.4).[9] Since 1995, the average age of the DoD civilian has risen from 44 to 46 years.

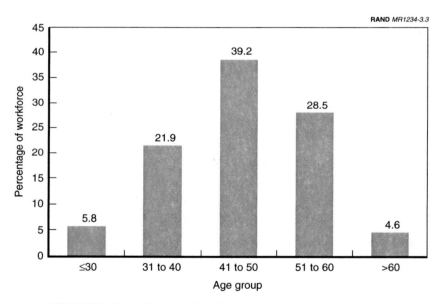

SOURCE: Defense Manpower Data Center (1999).

Figure 3.3—Distribution of Civilian Workforce, by Age Group, 1999

---

[9]Defense Manpower Data Center (2001).

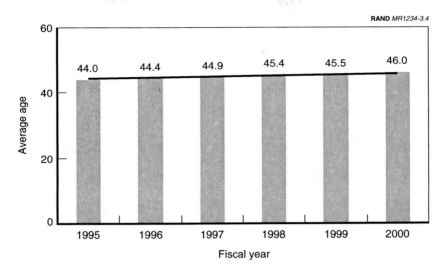

RAND *MR1234-3.4*

SOURCE: Defense Manpower Data Center (2001).

Figure 3.4—Average Age of DoD Civilian Workforce, 1995–2000

The Chancellor's office needs to develop a strategy of training and educating that is reflective of the learning behavior of a more mature workforce. The Chancellor's office may also need to consider the payoff period of training certain age groups that have large representation among the workforce. Complicating matters further, the Chancellor's office faces the double task of creating a strategy for dealing with a very mature workforce as well as a strategy to train and educate the workforce that replaces the retiring workers.

In an overall sense, the combination of projected changing demands on the civilian workforce and the demographic trends in the civilian workforce (as well as in the larger U.S. workforce) suggests that the functions played by the Chancellor's office will increase in importance over the next decade. Although the Chancellor's office is not responsible for recruiting or retaining the DoD's civil service workforce, its role in improving the quality of ET&D programs may assist the DoD's recruitment and retention efforts. In the future, the DoD is expected to compete in a market that pays a premium for high-tech skills that are highly critical for the DoD's future. The existence of strong ET&D programs, under the aegis of the Chancellor's office, will be useful tools in the DoD's recruitment and retention of higher skilled workers.

LEGISLATIVE DEVELOPMENTS: GOVERNMENT PERFORMANCE AND RESULTS ACT

In the 1990s, Congress passed several pieces of legislation that address waste and inefficiency, increase program effectiveness, and improve the internal management of the federal government. Laws along these lines include the Chief Financial Officers (CFO) Act of 1990, the Clinger-Cohen Information Technology Reform Act of 1996 and, most important, the GPRA of 1993. Each law has contributed to shifting the focus in federal agency operations away from inputs and process and toward outcomes and results.

The GPRA directs the 24 largest federal agencies (which includes the DoD) to submit five-year strategic plans as well as annual performance plans alongside their budget requests to Congress. The GPRA is relevant to the Chancellor's office because of its centerpiece strategic planning component that aims to help federal agencies develop a results-oriented focus. It requires that agency plans have

- A comprehensive mission statement,

- A description of general goals and objectives,

- A description of the means and strategies that will be used to achieve the goals and objectives,

- A description of the relationship between performance goals in the annual performance plan and the general goals and objectives in the strategic plan,

- Identification of key external factors that could affect achievement of the general goals and objectives, and

- A description of program evaluations used, including a schedule for future evaluations.[10]

---

[10]OMB (1998).

The GPRA mandates that agencies work to ensure that all operations and functions contribute to the strategic goals of the organization, although how agencies cascade accountability and responsibility for making the linkage between departmentwide strategic goals and lower-level agency goals differs considerably across the federal government. The implementation literature from the General Accounting Office (GAO) recommends that subordinate agencies such as the Chancellor's office take the initiative to coordinate their efforts with the strategic departmental goals and mission so that program efforts work synergistically.[11] The annual performance plan requirement of the GPRA offers the federal agency the opportunity to make the link between long-term strategic plans for the agency and daily activities of managers and staff. Each annual plan must include performance targets for all activities included in agency budget requests, a description of resources that will be used to meet the targets, and a discussion of how results will be measured.[12]

Federal agencies affected by the GPRA have made slow progress toward fulfilling the GPRA requirements, as they have struggled to articulate and define adequately their mission and the appropriate organizational performance measurement indicators. Coordination of cross-cutting programs in the federal government has proven difficult, as has the development of the necessary information systems required for reporting agency results.[13] The GAO and the OMB have provided feedback and guidance to agencies since the bill's inception, and the Congressional Government Oversight Committee has overseen the GPRA's implementation. But some good examples have also emerged. Common strengths of highly regarded plans include a clear mission statement and extensive consultation with stakeholders, a strong relationship between general goals and annual performance goals, clear recognition of external factors, and a solid plan for program evaluations.[14]

The Department of Defense employed its *Quadrennial Defense Review* report of 1997, along with supplementary documentation, as its

---

[11]GAO (1999b).

[12]GAO (1996).

[13]GAO (1998).

[14]Armey et al. (1997).

overall strategic plan to fulfill the provisions of the GPRA. A preliminary assessment of the strategic plan by the GAO noted that the DoD had met the six statutory requirements of the Results Act and included a concise mission statement as well as adequately defined general goals and objectives covering the DoD's major functions and operations.[15] The GAO recommended several improvements but, most of all, suggested the inclusion of more "comprehensive discussions of each of the required components."[16] Subsequently, the GAO assessed the compliance of the DoD's 1998 and 1999 Annual Performance Plans with the GPRA in a more critical fashion. The main objections included too high a level of explanation of "intended performance and associated qualitative and quantitative measures,"[17] a lack of adequate and reliable sources of data for performance measurement, and a lack of a discussion of the link between performance information and assessment of mission outcomes.[18]

The GPRA and the consequent effort to ensure its implementation offer a special opportunity for the Chancellor's office, in that they highlight the importance of strategic planning and validate the need for it at the level of subordinate agencies. Moreover, the assessments by the GAO help ensure that a well-crafted and appropriate strategic plan for the ET&D of DoD civilians will attract attention and contribute to the conditions for making its implementation successful.

TRENDS IN HIGHER EDUCATION QUALITY ASSURANCE

The interest in assessing quality and productivity within the institutions and programs under the purview of the Chancellor's office parallels similar interests in higher education. Several factors have influenced views toward quality assurance and productivity assessment in higher education over time, both in terms of how institutions view the process and from the point of view of external oversight. Public (and legislative) interest in ensuring accountability in public spending, the trend toward adoption of business practices in

---

[15]GAO (1997d).

[16]GAO, (1997d), p. 5.

[17]GAO (1998), p. 4.

[18]GAO (1999b).

the education sector, and the pressure on educational institutions to engage in self-improvement constitute some of the key influences. New technology (distance education) and globalization have also affected education. In many ways, the same influences and trends that have had an effect on higher education also have affected the federal government, including the DoD.

Historically, regional accrediting agencies have acted as the primary sources of quality assurance in higher education. They certify that individual institutions meet minimal levels of quality. In addition, specialized accrediting agencies certify specialized institutions and programs within institutions. However, numerous other approaches to quality assurance in higher education have surfaced. As these approaches have potential application for the Chancellor's office, they are also discussed below.[19]

Accreditation

The eight regional accrediting agencies, along with the almost 50 specialized and professional accreditation associations, operate as a form of voluntary peer evaluation. Accreditation has two primary purposes: (1) "to detect, eliminate and prevent fraud and abuse" (assure a minimal level of quality); and (2) "to assure adequate standardization of what an academic credit represents to facilitate transfer of credit from one institution to another."[20] At the same time, accreditation has the goal of enabling quality improvement at institutions through self-reflection. The coexistence of quality assurance and quality improvement roles produces an inherent tension. One requires the accrediting agency to act as an external monitor or judge of the higher education institution, and the other suggests that the agency play a role of a colleague of the institution.

Many accrediting agencies have taken a second look at the way they do business, with the Western Association of Schools and Colleges (WASC) considered by many to be at the forefront of the movement. Recognizing that students take courses at multiple institutions or

---

[19]For a more thorough discussion of approaches to quality assurance in higher education, see Gates et al. (2001).

[20]Glidden (1998).

transfer from a community college where they filled their general education requirements, and recognizing that students are increasingly
combining distance- and site-based learning, WASC has attempted
to make accreditation more flexible and relevant to what both students and institutions want to achieve.

Accountability

As higher education has become increasingly complex and large, and
the cost of delivering education has climbed, concern has grown
about the gap between the expectations of the public and the education that institutions of higher learning provide. In response to esca-
lating costs, state policymakers are adopting indicator systems (using
performance measures) as a way to help allocate funds, monitor the
overall condition of the sector, identify methods to improve the delivery of education, provide consumers with more information with
which to make informed choices, and better link higher education to
state priorities and goals.[21] Early interest in assessment and accountability led to more decentralization and gave institutions a
great deal of flexibility in measuring quality. However, over time,
state legislators have grown increasingly more specific in demanding
that institutions demonstrate the way public resources are being
spent.

Many states have adopted indicator systems as a way for institutions
to document performance. Some states have linked indicators to resource allocation, and many (with Tennessee probably the best
known) publish report cards so that the state government officials,
citizens, and employers can compare institutions across certain dimensions. Indicators can address both administrative and academic
issues. They typically measure such things as admission standards
and the number of entering students meeting those standards; re-
mediation activities and effectiveness; enrollment, retention, and
graduation data by gender, ethnicity, and program; number of student credit hours; and transfer rates.[22]

---

[21]Ruppert (1995).

[22]Ruppert (1995).

Portfolio

A new form of quality assessment consists of an institution or a group of institutions constructing institutional portfolios to document educational outcomes they produce and the methods used for achieving those outcomes. In one case, a group of six urban universities work together to share best practices among themselves and to demonstrate their accomplishments to the others.[23] This particular effort focuses on the distinct set of characteristics and constraints shared by urban universities, but groups of other types of institutions have undertaken similar efforts.

Academic Audit

Although relatively untested in the United States, the academic audit has seen use abroad, for example, in the United Kingdom, Hong Kong, and New Zealand. Like accreditation, academic audit evaluates the whole institution. However, it differs greatly from accreditation in that it does not aim for a comprehensive review. Instead, the focus of the audit is on an institution's own processes for measuring and improving academic quality. The objective of the audit is to ensure that institutions have such processes in place and thus can engage in ongoing self-improvement. The reviewers typically assess a few key processes identified by the institution—the processes could relate to the quality of a wide range of issues, including mission, organization, policies, resources, and research.[24] The institution itself is responsible for conducting the quality assessment according to these procedures.

Approaches in Business

The Balanced Scorecard and Malcolm Baldrige National Quality Award are the most prominent current tools adopted from the business sector to measure and ensure quality in higher education. Both of these approaches involve process evaluation rather than or in addition to a more traditional standards-based outcome assessment.

---

[23]*Urban Universities Portfolio Project.*
[24]Dill (2000), p. 2.

The Balanced Scorecard approach goes beyond traditional measures of financial success to include multiple measures of performance. Additional domains considered in this approach include the customer perspective (retention, satisfaction, and number eligible who participate) as well as the internal business process perspective (time to process, response time) and the innovative and growth perspective (infrastructure in place to grow, technology expenditures, staff retention and satisfaction).[25] The Malcolm Baldrige National Quality Award, previously awarded only in business, now also considers applicants in the higher education sector. The criteria for the Malcolm Baldrige award in higher education mirror those historically used for the business award and include assessments in the following domains: leadership, strategic planning, student and stakeholder focus, information and analysis, faculty and staff focus, educational and support process management, and school performance results. Assessments within each domain take place along two dimensions: approach/development and results.[26]

Performance Measurement and Distance Education

As distance learning becomes more prevalent, the higher education community has contemplated the need to develop new modes of quality assurance and new standards for measuring performance. Distance providers cut across state and regional boundaries that have historically guided state accountability programs and accrediting agencies' spheres of responsibility. Advances in technology have led to increased examples of education provision cutting across global boundaries as well. Countries must decide whether to rely on the quality assurance practices of the provider country or of their own. Creating standards and allowing flexible delivery causes a special tension within the global marketplace. An additional challenge stems from the fact that web-based providers do not offer the same kind of faculty or student experiences typically measured by current quality assurance methods. As a result, distance learning is forcing education providers to distill the fundamental goals from the education process. Among other things, the challenge of assessing dis-

----

[25]Haine (1999).

[26]Malcolm Baldrige Quality Award Program (1999).

tance learning outcomes has renewed interest in the concept of student competencies.[27]

The degree of experimentation and variety of approaches used for quality and productivity assessment in higher education reflect some of the fundamental choices the Chancellor's office must make in devising a strategy for similar assessments. For example, is the Chancellor's office in the business of certifying the competencies of students, assessing the educational outcomes of the institutions providing the education, or certifying the processes that the institutions themselves use to evaluate their own performance? To what extent should the Chancellor's office provide information and guidelines but delegate the actual quality assurance process to the institutions? Regardless of the answers to these fundamental questions, the experience of higher education suggests that organizations in the business of assessing academic quality and productivity always face a changing set of external pressures. As a result, they must adopt a flexible approach and be willing to continuously adjust the assessment approach to respond to changes in the external environment.

_____

[27]The premise of competency-based education is that students should be certified on the basis of what they know and can do, rather than on the basis of the courses they take. With competency-based education, the focus of assessment shifts from the provider of education to the student.

Chapter Four

KEY CHALLENGES IN DoD CIVILIAN EDUCATION AND WORKFORCE PLANNING

Having considered some of the major trends in the environment of the Chancellor's office, we now consider the key characteristics of DoD civilian ET&D. Key stakeholders in DoD civilian ET&D include

- Customers—the approximately 700,000 civil service employees working for the DoD, their managers, the organizations employing them, and other organizations interested in the skill level of the DoD workforce, and

- Providers—organizations (both within and outside the DoD) providing education, training, and development opportunities related to employment of DoD civilians.[1]

Civilian ET&D is embedded within various civilian workforce management systems (e.g., Competitive Service, Excepted Service, and Non-Appropriated Fund employee systems) that must balance the needs of the DoD with the skills of the workforce through classification, recruiting, promotion, training, education, compensation, acculturation, and retention/separation policies. This larger system thus provides an important context for the ET&D system.

This chapter describes DoD civilian ET&D in general, and particularly how the Chancellor's office fits into the DoD ET&D system. We

---

[1]In contrast to professional military education, training, and development, DoD civilian ET&D is not well specified at more detailed levels of description. There is little uniformity across providers and stakeholders in terms of the procedures by which education and professional development are acquired and accounted for.

discuss civilian workforce and workforce planning issues to the extent that they influence the activities of the Chancellor's office.

DoD CIVILIAN EDUCATION, TRAINING, AND DEVELOPMENT

In October 1998, the DoD Office of the Chancellor for Education and Professional Development was established with the mission of being the principal advocate for the academic quality and cost-effectiveness of all DoD institutions, programs, and courses of instruction that provide education or professional development for DoD civilians. As such, the Office of the Chancellor is neither a direct consumer nor a producer of ET&D activities but rather a resource available to the key customers and providers. It must use whatever tools it has to help bring about improvements in civilian education and professional development to the satisfaction of all stakeholders involved.

The system with which the Chancellor's office is associated is a complicated one. First, the network of provider organizations is heterogeneous. The OSD sponsors more than 20 institutions and numerous programs and courses of instruction serving DoD civilians.[2] Countless other courses and programs for DoD civilian personnel are available through institutions run by the Army, Navy, Air Force, and Marine Corps, as well as through providers outside the DoD. Some of these institutions are accredited, and some of the accredited institutions offer academic degree programs.

The provider network is heterogeneous not only in terms of its organizational structure but also with respect to the content of educational offerings. Provider organizations within the office's area of interest deliver technical training, professional development, and

---

[2]The institutions include the DoD Polygraph Institute, the Defense Equal Opportunity Management Institute, and the National Imagery and Mapping College among others. Programs, of which there are many, include the Defense Leadership and Management Program, the Defense Information Systems Agency Leadership Development Program, Family Advocacy Staff Training, and Commissary Operations Training. Readers interested in more information on specific institutions, programs, and courses under consideration by the Chancellor's office are referred to Baldwin (1998), and Office of the Assistant Secretary of Defense for Force Management Policy (1997).

postsecondary education up through the graduate level to DoD civilians in disciplines including information technology, financial management, acquisition, business management, security and intelligence, engineering, and health. Because of the range of opportunities offered, the populations served by the organizations vary and so do their sponsors. The wide variety of ET&D programs presents challenges in terms of planning and managing the system and complicates the formation of any uniform set of criteria for evaluating quality and cost-effectiveness.

The customer dimension of the system is equally complicated because of the sheer number of potential learners and the structure within which they work and seek to acquire education. The DoD civilian workforce, which constitutes the pool from which potential learners are drawn, is approximately 700,000. Most employees work in the United States, but some DoD civilians are stationed abroad. The sheer size of the system's potential consumer population complicates the management and delivery of ET&D and the tracking of student performance before, during, and after the educational component. Such tracking facilitates the assessment of the quality and cost-effectiveness of such activities.

Another challenge stems from the fact that there are multiple organizations, both within and outside the DoD, that have an interest in or influence over DoD civilian ET&D activities. Figure 4.1 illustrates this point.

The figure suggests that federal legislation and other federal agencies, nationally recognized accrediting organizations, and the Secretary of Defense all have high-level influence over the content, structure, and quality of the system. For example, federal law places a restriction on employee training for the purpose of obtaining an academic degree.[3] Generally, federal agencies may provide or fund such training to recruit or retain employees in occupations having a shortage of qualified personnel. Also, the Department of Defense may provide or fund such training if it is a part of a planned, systematic, and coordinated program of professional development endorsed by the Department of Defense. Nationally recognized

---

[3]Section 4107, Title 5, United States Code.

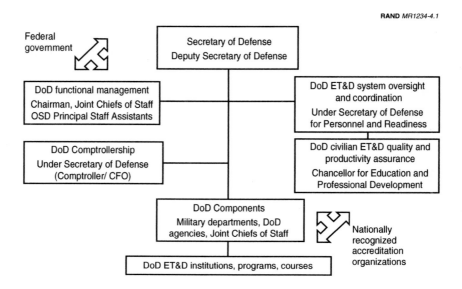

Figure 4.1—Key Stakeholders in DoD Civilian Education, Training, and Development

accrediting organizations also influence the DoD ET&D system. Any course of postsecondary education delivered through classroom, electronic, or other means must be administered or conducted by an institution recognized under standards implemented by a national or regional accrediting body. Another piece of legislation, the Government Performance and Results Act, has focused attention on assessing the quality and cost-effectiveness of all government activities. DoD civilian ET&D is one of many activities subject to such scrutiny.

DoD functional sponsors for institutions and programs are responsible for functional policy of some institutions and programs: determining what needs to be trained at what level. In some cases, they may also be resource sponsors responsible for allocating financial resources earmarked for education, training, or development. DoD component and agency heads, who have ultimate responsibility for the workforce planning and management, have a direct interest in the provision of ET&D. They often provide their own courses and programs and sometimes sponsor their own institutions. The Under

Secretary of Defense for Personnel and Readiness (USD (P&R)) has oversight and responsibility for developing policies, plans, and programs relating to education, training, and development of the Total Force. Finally, the Chancellor's office is responsible for ensuring the quality and cost-effectiveness of civilian ET&D activities.

Table 4.1 summarizes the role that these different organizational entities play in the ET&D system.

Although not all ET&D activities are provided by formal DoD-run educational institutions, these institutions provide a useful starting

Table 4.1

The Role of Organizational Entities in Education, Training, and Development

Organizational Entity	Role
Secretary of Defense, nationally recognized accrediting organizations, federal government	Influence over content, structure, and quality of the system
DoD functional management	Functional sponsor for education activities; responsible for functional policy for some institutions and programs—determining what needs to be trained at what level
DoD Comptrollership	Allocates financial resources in support of ET&D
USD (P&R)	Oversight and coordinating responsibility for DoD ET&D
Chancellor for Education and Professional Development	Principal advocate for quality and cost-effectiveness of education and professional development activities
DoD Component heads	Responsibility for workforce planning and management; may provide courses, programs, or institutions; ultimate source of line management authority over institutions and programs; often will delegate this responsibility to command sponsors; provide nonfinancial resources to institutions (facilities, equipment, personnel)

point for the assessment of quality and cost-effectiveness because they are clearly identifiable and therefore the easiest to consider.

Figure 4.2 depicts a bottom-up view of the ET&D system from the perspective of the formal provider institutions.[4] Each institution has a functional sponsor who is responsible for determining or approving the content of the curriculum. The institution's resource sponsor is responsible for providing the resources (dollars, facilities, and civilian and military personnel) to support the ET&D activities. The command sponsor of an institution is the organization to which the institution's director or commander officially reports. We should point out that a single organizational entity within the DoD may be responsible for more than one of the functions depicted in Figure 4.2. For example, the functional sponsor and the command sponsor may be the same. An institution may also have a board of visitors that provides advice on curriculum or operational issues.

To make the terminology used in this figure more concrete, consider the example of a specific school under the purview of the

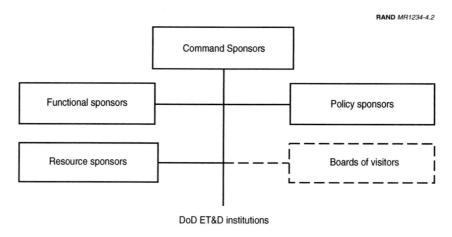

Figure 4.2—Structure of Responsibility for Provider Institutions

---

[4]As noted above, not all education, training, and development is provided by institutions.

Chancellor's office, the Defense Language Institute Foreign Language Center (DLIFLC). The functional sponsor is the Assistant Secretary of Defense (Command, Control, and Communications Intelligence) (ASD (C3I)), who heads the school's program policy committee and guides the development of the curriculum. DLIFLC resources come from the U.S. Army through the U.S. Army Training and Doctrine Command (TRADOC) comptroller, and thus TRADOC acts as the resource sponsor. TRADOC is also the source of direct reporting authority for DLIFLC. Deputy Commanding General, TRADOC, is the reporting senior for the Commandant, DLIFLC. Finally, the USD (P&R) is the policy sponsor for all education and professional development.

The Chancellor's office does not appear in Figure 4.2 because the office has no direct line management authority over the providers. However, the office's means of influence are no less real for being indirect. The Chancellor's office does have a measure of authority regarding the providers, for example, to collect information from them. Also, the charter of the Chancellor's office specifies a collaborative relationship with the functional sponsors of the institutions to ensure academic quality and cost-effectiveness. Although the Chancellor's office is not in a position to implement academic quality assurance measures, its recommendations to the functional sponsors can have a profound effect upon the providers, in the same way that the recommendations of the Inspector General to top bodies in the OSD can influence the way the services conduct their activities. The Chancellor's office also recommends standards to the USD (P&R) and the Secretary of Defense for implementation throughout the department.

WORKFORCE PLANNING AND MANAGEMENT CONSIDERATIONS

ET&D is just one element of a workforce planning and management system. The ET&D system, and thus the assessment of such a system, is influenced by civilian workforce characteristics as well as by workforce planning and management activities. To a large extent, education, training, and development are a means to improve the quality of the workforce and ultimately must be evaluated on that basis. In other words, the Chancellor's office is a resource for those in charge of workforce planning, as well as education, training, and development. The Chancellor's office can be most effective in achieving its mission by being closely integrated with that larger system.

One challenge facing the Chancellor's office is that although the OUSD (P&R) is ultimately responsible for civilian workforce planning, it carries out functions through various principal staff. Hence, no single entity determines what the provider institutions should offer. The military services and some DoD agencies are responsible for planning for their civilian employees. The Principal Staff Assistants in OSD have a planning role in some specialized areas, such as acquisition or comptroller. In addition, the Office of the Deputy Assistant Secretary of Defense for Civilian Personnel Policy is responsible for a variety of issues influencing civilian personnel, including planning and management of the civilian workforce.

Figure 4.3 shows the position of the Chancellor's office in the formal reporting hierarchy of DoD. The Chancellor reports to USD (P&R) through the Defense Human Resources Activity, which is coordinated by the Deputy Under Secretary of Defense for Program Integration. It is worth noting that the DASD (CPP), who has significant responsibility for DoD civilian workforce policy and planning, is also in the USD (P&R) chain of command but reports to USD (P&R) through the ASD (FMP). In other words, the organizational link between the Chancellor's office and the myriad entities with responsibility for some aspect of workforce planning (military component heads, DASD (CPP), etc.) is indirect.

CIVILIAN WORKFORCE PLANNING

The system of civilian workforce planning faces several challenges in attempting to address perceived problems with the quality of the civilian workforce. Although increased attention on improving the quality of ET&D may help, the link between the quality of ET&D on the one hand and the quality of the workforce on the other is confounded by several factors.

The major problem is that current education, training, and development offerings are usually based on a vague sense of what is needed

RAND *MR1234-4.3*

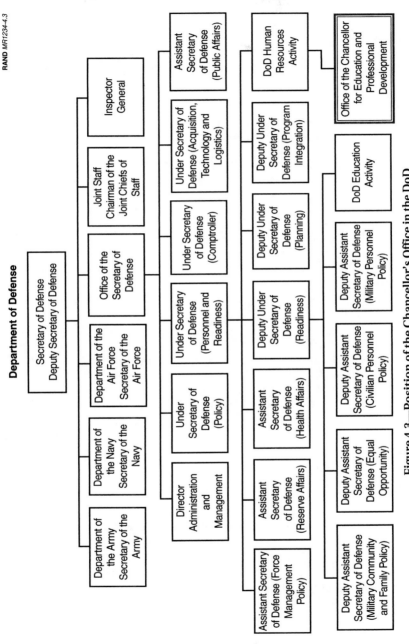

Figure 4.3—Position of the Chancellor's Office in the DoD

rather than on an analysis of the gaps between current or projected workforce characteristics and required workforce characteristics. Education, training, and development can help address the perceived quality problem only if the source of the problem is well defined and if the education activities are specifically designed to address it. Although some degree of workforce planning is going on at the highest levels of the DoD or within OUSD (P&R), analyses of civilian workforce needs and consideration of how ET&D might address those needs are not comprehensive.

Even if ET&D is integrated with workforce planning so that the content of the education activities addresses identified skills gaps, workforce quality might not improve. This is because the quality of the workforce (or more specifically the outcomes produced by that workforce) is also affected by the incentives that employees have to obtain and make use of training and development. Expectancy theory (Steers et al., 1996) emphasizes that employees will be motivated to behave in a specific way when (1) they believe that they are able to perform at the desired level, (2) they believe that certain levels of performance will lead to desired outcomes, and (3) these outcomes are of some value to the employees.

Education, training, and development can influence employees' confidence in their ability to perform by providing them with the skills and knowledge required. However, if the link between prospects for promotion and educational experiences is unclear, there is less motivation for workers to seek ET&D that could promote better job performance. Even if such incentives exist, when career paths are not closely integrated with education, it is difficult to relate specific courses to advancement. If workforce planning is not well integrated with education and developmental incentives, implementation of workforce improvement becomes more difficult.

Another problem is best seen in contrast with the military personnel system. The civil service follows the model of rank in position, whereas the military follows a model of rank in person. The rank in position model hinders workforce planning because people cannot be moved around as easily or trained to do several jobs. This lack of "fungibility" severely constrains the flexibility of the workforce in times of great change and uncertainty and again reduces the incentives for workers to acquire additional education. The military and civilian cases also differ in that DoD military personnel requirements and resources are centrally managed, whereas DoD civilian requirements and resources are not centrally managed, although DoD functional management and components may vary somewhat in the latter regard. As a result, decisionmaking regarding civilian workforce management is decentralized for the most part in the DoD.

KEY CHALLENGES IN DoD CIVILIAN EDUCATION, TRAINING, AND DEVELOPMENT

As the above makes clear, the Chancellor's office faces numerous challenges. Although the office's mission is relatively narrow—to be the principal advocate for the academic quality and cost-effectiveness of all DoD institutions, programs, and courses of instruction that provide education or professional development for DoD civilians—the motivation for establishment of the office reflects a much larger concern about the quality of the DoD civilian workforce. Improving the quality of ET&D can and should help improve the quality of the civilian workforce, but ET&D is just one element of a much larger workforce planning strategy. To maximize the effect of its efforts, the Chancellor's office should encourage the development of a conceptual framework to articulate the overarching educational needs of the DoD and persuade the functional and resource sponsors to adequately resource the changes outlined. This challenge stands apart from the no-less-difficult but more technical question of how the Chancellor's office should promote academic quality and cost-effectiveness given its limited authority over funds, institutions, programs, and courses of instruction. The office does not, for example, have the powers that a Chancellor in academic circles typically has to approve or disband academic programs.

In sum, there are two categories of challenges facing DoD civilian ET&D: those facing the civilian workforce planning system in using ET&D as a tool to improve the workforce and those facing the Chancellor's office as it develops a strategy to assess the quality and cost-effectiveness of education, training, and development.

Challenges Facing the Civilian Workforce Planning System

- Changing nature of the work to be performed,

- Loose integration between workforce planning, education, and employee reward systems,

- An aging consumer population, the specter of mass retirements, and the problem of ensuring that replacements have similarly high qualifications, and

- Few incentives for workers to acquire education, training, and development.

Challenges Facing the Chancellor's Office

- Lack of an existing conceptual framework for workforce planning to guide the Chancellor's office,

- A Chancellor's office with minimal direct authority,

- A large and geographically dispersed consumer population,

- Multiple and diverse stakeholders in DoD civilian ET&D with uneven commitments to ET&D,

- Dramatic difference among provider institutions in terms of focus, population served, and sponsors, and

- Programs and courses of instruction ranging from technical training to professional development to graduate education.

The preceding should not be taken as an indication that the Chancellor's office is in an untenable organizational position. From the perspective of the glass being half-empty, the unique position of the Chancellor's office on the organizational chart and the presence of a multitude of stakeholders constrains its ability to implement its recommendations. However, those multiple stakeholders may provide the mechanism through which the office's recommendations can find multiple proponents.

The multiple stakeholders include the Secretary of Defense and the individual service secretaries who have the power to review, modify, and prioritize the requirements and programs put forth by the services in the planning and programming phases of the Planning, Programming, and Budgeting System. They also have the most direct interest in the ideas put forth by the Chancellor's office, because education, training, and development of the civilian DoD workforce is, ultimately, one of their responsibilities. The Chairman of the Joint Chiefs of Staff (CJCS) is another relevant stakeholder and, in view of the important supporting role of the DoD civilians in fulfilling the goals outlined in *JV 2010* and *JV 2020*, has an interest in the educational development of the civilian DoD workforce. Although the CJCS cannot be the central proponent for the recommendations issued by the Chancellor's office, his support can give the Chancellor's office additional weight in intra-DoD resource identification and management processes. Thus, in an overall sense, the presence of so many stakeholders can amplify the office's recommendations. Working effectively with so many interested parties will require skill and political savvy but it may lead to an effective, if indirect, effect on DoD civilian ET&D.

In the next chapter, we demonstrate how we used the challenges enumerated here to identify similar organizations in higher education, business, and government that could yield lessons in strategic planning with particular relevance to the concerns of the Chancellor's office.

Chapter Five

IDENTIFYING AND INVESTIGATING BEST-PRACTICE ORGANIZATIONS

In this chapter, we discuss best practices among organizations that share at least some of the same challenges facing the Chancellor's office. Those organizations can be divided into seven general classes:

- Accrediting agencies,

- Corporate universities and human resources departments,

- DoD professional military education, training, and development systems,

- Other federal agencies,

- Higher education systems and universities,

- Professional societies and labor unions, and

- State boards of higher education.

Within each class, we identified one or more best practice cases to study. The case studies were based either on the available literature or on intensive site visits. Case studies based on the literature are reported in Appendix B. Appendix C contains detailed notes from the site visits.

We chose to conduct the site visits at best-practice institutions that shared the most similarities with the Chancellor's office based on a subjective assessment of the challenges they faced (as outlined in Chapter Four). The resulting matrix was used to help identify organizations that most resembled the Chancellor's office. We conducted site visits with best-practice institutions in the top two categories.

The matrix that guided the site visits is shown in Table 5.1. The rows are the two sets of challenges—workforce planning challenges and challenges facing the Chancellor's office—that were discussed in the previous chapters.

From Table 5.1, it is clear that the most fruitful site visits were likely to come from other federal agencies and state boards of higher education.[1] The site visits chosen from these areas—the Department of Transportation and the state boards of higher education in Kentucky and Texas—are documented in Appendix C.

We consulted three sources for nominations of federal agencies exhibiting best practices in strategic planning: the literature on strategic planning in corporate education, an expert in federal management issues at the GAO, and a congressional review of the first round of strategic plans released in 1997. The Department of Transportation was rated among the best by all three sources.

The case for state boards was more equivocal. There are two basic types of state boards: coordinating boards and governing boards.[2] The types are similar in that their primary purpose is to mediate between the desires of politicians and other interested parties who would like to influence higher education and the institutions of higher education themselves. The primary differences are that governing boards have fiduciary responsibility for all public institutions in the state and have formal status in the state constitution. Generally, they also have the power to appoint institutional presidents and system Chancellors, set faculty personnel policy, and determine tuition policies. Coordinating boards do not have fiduciary responsibility, status in the state constitution, or the authority to appoint institution presidents, set faculty policies, or determine tuition

---

[1]In our matrix, corporate universities ranked a distant third. Nonetheless, readers interested in strategic planning for business in general are referred to Mintzberg and Lampel (1999); and Mintzberg, Ahlstrand, and Lampel (1998).

[2]For a detailed description of the types of state boards including a classification of states, see Education Commission of the States (1997).

Table 5.1

Assessing Similarity to the Situation of the Chancellor's Office

Challenge	Other Federal Agencies	State Boards of Higher Education	Human Resources Departments, Corporate Universities	Higher Education Systems, Universities	Professional Societies, Labor Unions	DoD Professional Military ET&D Systems	Accrediting Agencies
Changing work	+	0	+	–	+	+	–
Integration of planning and education	+	0	0	0	–	–	–
Aging workforce	+	0	0	–	–	–	–
Few incentives for education	+	+	0	0	–	–	–
No conceptual framework	0	–	–	+	–	–	+
Chancellor's authority	+	+	–	0	+	–	+
Large consumer base	0	+	+	0	0	+	–
Multiple stakeholders	0	+	–	0	0	0	–
Diverse providers	+	+	–	0	–	–	–
Training to education	+	0	+	–	0	0	0
Total points	**+7**	**+4**	**–1**	**–2**	**–3**	**–4**	**–5**

NOTES: + indicates that there are likely to be useful similarities between organizations of that type and the chancellor's office. 0 means that there might be useful similarities. – indicates dissimilarities in that dimension are unlikely to produce anything useful for the chancellor's office. Items with the same score were ranked according to number of +s.

policies.[3] Coordinating boards have the authority either to approve academic programs or to review and make recommendations to institutional governing boards.

As the Chancellor's office has neither fiduciary responsibility over institutions nor the power to appoint institutional leaders, we elected to visit state higher education coordinating boards rather than governing boards. Both the Texas and the Kentucky boards are considered regulatory coordinating boards because they have the authority to approve academic programs. In other words, they perform more than just an advisory function.

Experts in higher education identified the boards in Kentucky and Texas as leading-edge coordinating boards in terms of their strategic planning efforts. Unlike the case for the Department of Transportation, there was not clear consensus across the six experts we consulted about higher education coordinating boards as to which boards exhibited the best strategic planning processes and outcomes. Several experts recommended the Illinois Board of Higher Education in addition to the boards in Texas and Kentucky. Our ability to gain access to key decisionmakers on the boards in Texas and Kentucky was one of several factors that influenced our final selection. Another factor was that Texas was the only board cited that was undergoing a fundamental review of its strategic plan, allowing us to learn firsthand about the issues faced by a mature higher education coordinating board. Moreover, the higher education system in Texas is one of the few that approaches the size and scope of the universe of the Chancellor's office. In contrast, the board in Kentucky recently underwent a change in leadership to deal with a virtual crisis in higher education. A preliminary look at Kentucky revealed many parallels with the situation faced by the Chancellor's office and thus the potential for many useful lessons in strategic planning.

---

[3]Twenty-four states have governing boards. These tend to be states with relatively small, homogenous populations such as Utah and North Carolina. Larger states such as Wisconsin also have governing boards. Twenty-four states have coordinating boards. Coordinating boards tend to be in states with a large or heterogeneous population or in states with a large private sector. Michigan and Delaware have neither a governing nor a coordinating board, only a planning agency.

The following ten cases selected for the literature reviews were also identified mainly based on expert opinion and cover the remaining broad classes of organizations listed at the start of this chapter:

Accrediting agencies

- WASC

Corporate universities, human resources departments

- Fidelity Institutional Retirement Services Company (FIRSCo's) Service Delivery University (SDU)

Other federal agencies

- The Department of Education
- The Social Security Administration

Higher education systems and universities

- The University System of Georgia
- California State University (CSU)
- The California Master Plan

DoD professional military education, training, and development systems

- The Army system

Professional societies, labor unions

- The American Medical Association (AMA)

In addition to the above cases, we researched the Quality Assurance Agency (QAA), an organization in the United Kingdom funded mainly by subscriptions from universities and colleges to review the performance of the higher education institutions in the British system. We chose to look at the QAA because of the similarity of its mission to that of the Chancellor's office.

The full findings from our literature reviews are presented in Appendix B. In the next chapter, we discuss the key insights gained from the case studies and consider their appropriateness as strategies for the Chancellor's office.

Chapter Six

"GOLDEN NUGGETS" FOR THE CHANCELLOR'S OFFICE

Our case studies have allowed us to identify a number of potential approaches to addressing the challenges outlined in Chapters Four and Five. This chapter focuses on lessons that were most salient and potentially applicable to the Chancellor's office. (See Appendices B and C for the complete case study reports.)

Our findings speak to three of the components of strategic planning identified in Chapter Two—vision, strategies, and governance. Note that we do not recommend that the Chancellor's office adopt complete strategic or performance planning models. Rather, we have identified discrete insights that the Chancellor's office can use during its strategic planning effort. We segregated the findings into three categories: near-term actions to be considered for the next two to three years, medium-term strategies for the next five years, and strategies that should be employed over the lifetime of the office.

We also have identified strategies related to defense civilian workforce planning. Those strategies currently lie outside the charter of the Chancellor's office but should be considered as the Chancellor's office continues to define its role in DoD civilian ET&D.

NEAR-TERM ACTIONS

Become the Information Center

Several organizations we studied, particularly state higher education coordinating boards, shared the problems of minimal authority faced by the Chancellor's office. Many of these organizations compensated for their lack of authority by developing a reputation as the primary source of quality information about education. This method has been employed effectively by the Learning and Development Council in the Department of Transportation (DoT), the AMA, the Texas Higher Education Coordinating Board, and the Kentucky Council for Postsecondary Education (CPE). In developing the California Master Plan, multiple task forces spent one year doing massive data collection and analysis of enrollment trends, institutional capacity and area needs, and the costs of higher education (in addition to other activities). In Kentucky, information is considered a particularly important source of power, used to understand the strengths and vulnerabilities of institutions and to keep them "on their toes." The Chancellor's office could consider such an approach as a fourth model of identity or purpose in addition to the three listed in Chapter Two—*director, expert,* and *facilitator.* Although somewhat related to the expert model, this model would place more emphasis on the nature of the information possessed by the Chancellor's office as opposed to the perceived characteristics of the office itself.

Include Stakeholders in Strategy Development

The most prevalent strategy for making decisions that affect multiple stakeholders is to include the stakeholders in the decisionmaking process. WASC—one of the leading accrediting agencies—invited leading thinkers to submit "concept papers" about effectiveness, then developed a dialog among stakeholders to promote cooperation among institutions and greater synergy across a system of otherwise competing institutions. Likewise, the task forces that contributed to the development of the California Master Plan drew representatives from the University of California, state colleges, junior colleges, the State Board of Education, K–12 education, and the independent colleges and universities, as well as the legislature and other state agencies.

The DoT Learning and Development Council (LDC) uses this strategy by bringing together representatives from all the operating administrations' (OAs') human resources offices to provide recommendations and guidance for overall learning and development policies. Involvement in the LDC helps OAs feel some ownership of the recommended policies and strategies. For similar reasons, the Higher Education Coordinating Board in Texas has promoted broad participation in the process of building a new strategic plan. Finally, the Kentucky CPE sees the involvement of stakeholders as a valuable avenue for "trading stories" and has therefore established a permanent advisory committee.

Define Specific Strategies for Stakeholder Groups

To help ensure the effectiveness of its strategic plan, the Chancellor's office should specify strategies to address the different needs and priorities of its stakeholder groups. Failure to do so would weaken the usefulness of the plan. For instance, the overall learning plan for DoT is too generic to be useful to the OAs, so they must tailor it to fit their purposes. In contrast, the strategic plan for the CSU system emphasizes shared responsibility while specifying what faculty and administrators will do, what will be asked of students and the state, and how the different constituencies will benefit in the end. In a similar vein, WASC is revising its accreditation standards using a very inclusive, experimental process. It is trying to move beyond simply measuring inputs to developing measures more closely linked to individual campus goals. The campuses within its purview are very involved in the process of developing new standards and are exploring different methods, including portfolios.

Differentiate Among the Multiple ET&D Missions

The Chancellor's office will face a number of critical decisions as it establishes governance arrangements to implement its strategic plan. Paying attention to the governance system is most critical at the office's formative stage. It also will be important at later stages, when the office contemplates whether different kinds of governance arrangements might improve the institution's ability to carry out its mission.

Some of the institutions under the purview of the Chancellor's office are undergraduate-degree-granting institutions. Others are specific programs in skill training such as intelligence. The initial mission distinctions the Chancellor's office makes will shape its subsequent relationships and decisions. For example, in the formulation of the

California Master Plan, when the liaison committee was able to segment the three systems of higher education (community colleges, state four-year universities, and doctoral institutions) by law, a set of governance arrangements for higher education in California were put in place that observers continue to find both effective and efficient.

Develop Assessment Criteria

A primary strategic need for the Chancellor's office is to find and reach agreement on assessment criteria, standards, and benchmarks for institutions offering ET&D to DoD civilians. Because of the centrality of this need to the mission of the Chancellor's office, RAND undertook a separate effort focused solely on approaches to the assessment of the quality and cost-effectiveness of education, training, and development.[1]

MEDIUM-TERM STRATEGIES

Gain Agreement for Specific Reporting Requirements

It will be important to formalize basic reporting requirements that will help the Chancellor's office carry out its functions. For instance, WASC requires that all institutions of higher education under its authority have mission statements and internal faculty governance procedures. The University of Georgia system requires that the institutions it governs reflect its priorities in their strategic plans. The institutions in the three systems of higher education in California all meet in legislative-like settings on a regular basis to review, advise, and make recommendations to their system headquarters and to the California Postsecondary Commission. There is agreement in the United Kingdom that the Quality Assurance Agency charged with performance review of higher education institutions will publish its results. This public reporting appears itself to have a significant effect on the behavior of the higher education institutions.

---

[1]See Gates et al. (2001).

Acquire a Role in the Program Approval Process

An office's ability to acquire legislative authority or gain legislative backing clearly increases its influence. In Texas, the board has the authority to approve or disapprove programs eligible for state funding and can recommend changes to the higher education funding formula or raise other issues to the legislature. However, the board recognizes that it must not be too aggressive in promoting its vision against the will of the institutions or the legislature, or it risks becoming irrelevant. In Kentucky, the CPE can also approve or close programs, and although the latter is rarely done, the ability to do so is considered to be of particular importance. It supplements this authority by using incentive funds to encourage changes. The CPE further benefits from the strong backing of its "education governor," and when possible, links education with other efforts (e.g., economic and workforce development).

Eliminate Governance Obstacles

As the Chancellor's office develops its programs, existing lines of authority may prove to be too complex or unclear. Under these circumstances, the Chancellor's office may wish to recommend remedies. By the mid-1990s, the AMA's members and the medical community at-large criticized the association's complicated and unclear governance system. The association formed a committee in 1998 to rework its governance structure. Whether the committee will generate actual changes remains to be seen, but the need to clarify governance arrangements has been identified.

LIFETIME STRATEGIES

Play a Flexible Role

As noted at the outset of this report, the context in which the Chancellor's office currently operates is changing in significant ways. In Texas, the role of the board has changed over time in response to new external circumstances. In times of economic growth, its role has been to slow growth in higher education and ensure that the growth is quality growth. In times of budget austerity, the board has promoted cost control. In other words, the board has served as a foil to the more extreme tendencies of the legislature and the institutions. This strategy is one that will be critical as the Chancellor's office works to define its role in DoD civilian ET&D and will remain important in assuring the survival of the office over the long term.

Use Different Strategies for Different Sets of Institutions

In implementing its strategic plan, the Chancellor's office will have to take into consideration the broad range of programs offered to DoD civilians. Faced with a similar situation, the Kentucky CPE has let go of trying to develop a single definition of quality and is focusing more on "fitness for purpose." Likewise, the higher education coordinating board in Texas uses fundamentally different approaches for two-year and four-year institutions, both in evaluations of quality and in funding formulas. And in Georgia, their Chancellor's office analyzed a number of different areas (e.g., enrollment, workforce trends, capital priorities) and identified unique performance targets for each campus.

This strategy could become cumbersome if it begins to lead to a different approach for each institution or program. To avoid this problem, the American Medical Association aggregates institutions under its purview by the type of education provided. This has resulted in several affiliated organizations over which AMA has some control. Each organization is responsible for some aspect of medical education. For instance, the Accreditation Council on Continuing Medical Education partakes in accrediting institutions that offer continuing medical programs for physicians, the Accreditation Council for Graduate Medical Education (ACGME) accredits medical residency programs, and so on. In past looks at the provider institutions serving DoD civilians,[2] it has been possible to employ a similar strategy by categorizing along a few dimensions—length of courses, whether the courses led to a degree, and accreditation status.

---

[2]See OASD (FMP) (1997).

Establish a Constituency for Reforms

If the Chancellor's office hopes to implement its recommendations over the long term, it must pursue and maintain the backing of key stakeholders. The human resources office at the DoT is trying to develop a performance consulting approach—a participatory role as opposed to a command and control mentality. The Texas board considers positive public perception to be one of its three main sources of power. And in Kentucky, the Kentucky Education Reform Act that reformed K–12 education is being used as a model for higher education, because it survived three governors by establishing a constituency for the changes. The president of the Kentucky CPE also meets monthly with the heads of the educational institutions to keep them engaged in the reform process. The Quality Assurance Agency in Great Britain employs a similar strategy. It promotes confidence in the quality of programs by involving all stakeholders in improving standards, providing information about standards and performance, and providing examples of model practice. The Chancellor's office could emulate these strategies both to encourage the implementation of its near-term recommendations and to bolster its future position.

INTEGRATION WITH WORKFORCE PLANNING STRATEGIES

We identified a number of collaborative strategies that currently lie outside the charter of the Chancellor's office but could enhance the quality and cost-effectiveness of ET&D if implemented. Those strategies are presented below and should be considered if the office's role is expanded.

Identify Salient Obstacles and Incentives for Members of the Workforce

Quality improvements in DoD civilian ET&D will lead to increased workforce participation only if the workforce is motivated to take advantage of available opportunities. A potential element of the future strategy of the Chancellor's office will therefore be to find incentives that will appropriately motivate the population and recommend ways to implement them. The council in Kentucky believes that the concept of higher pay for better education is potentially a strong motivator for its population, so it has supported an advertising campaign with the slogan "Education Pays" as its centerpiece.

In the workforce, managers may be indifferent to professional education and development or may even oppose it (if they mainly see it as time taken away from ongoing tasks). At FIRSCo, line managers support rather than oppose workers' professional development because a percentage of their annual bonus depends on the extent to which their employees have prepared and fulfilled professional development plans. To focus on this challenge, the Chancellor's office could try to identify key factors underlying the reasons DoD civilians take advantage of professional development opportunities less than private-sector employees do.[3]

Promote the Strategic Role of Education, Training, and Development

DoT's LDC realizes that it is critical to link strategic planning with learning and development. Making the link requires that line managers connect learning with the strategic plans required by the GPRA.[4] By emphasizing the connection between learning and mission performance, and stressing that learning is an investment and not an expense, the LDC is raising awareness of the importance of education and professional development. At FIRSCo, the SDU closely aligns its priorities with the corporation's major business missions. It aims to develop employees who understand the service delivery profit chain and the critical role they play in driving customer satisfaction and loyalty, which in turn are seen as drivers of profit and growth.

At a general level, this is a strategy the Chancellor's office may choose so as to highlight its crucial role in developing the necessary workforce to carry out the DoD's mission. Making a strong case for the effect that its policies can have on the overall performance of the DoD

---

[3]See Lee and Clery (1999).

[4]These critical relationships are outlined in Human Resources Development Council (1997).

may go a long way toward establishing a place for the Chancellor's office in the department.

Engage Sponsors in the Education, Training, and Development Effort

The Chancellor's office faces an important challenge in trying to increase sponsors' awareness of and commitment to DoD educational institutions. Clearly, building such commitment is key to enhancing the quality of the programs offered. At FIRSCo, primary responsibility for professional development rests with line managers—not with the human resources department. In addition, incentives are given to line managers to encourage professional development among workers. Further, higher-level managers carry out all the significant planning and decisionmaking roles at SDU, serving, for instance, as deans, advisory board members, and members of the teaching faculty for advanced courses. Similarly, DoT's LDC provides orientation training to OA managers to help make them aware of the strategic plan for professional development and how it relates to human resource issues. Although such changes are outside the current scope of its mission, the Chancellor's office could encourage moves in this direction by working closely with the functional sponsors of the institutions and with the Office of the DASD (CPP).

Promote a Demand-Driven System Through Coordination of Workforce Planning, Education, and Incentive Systems

The Chancellor could potentially cooperate with the USD (P&R) and the DASD (CPP) to integrate assessments of the quality of ET&D into civilian workforce planning. For civilians in the DoD, the degree of integration between workforce planning, ET&D, and incentive systems in career paths varies by career field. In the acquisitions field, there is strong integration; however, for most other career fields, coordination between these three domains is largely lacking.

One result of a lack of integration between workforce planning, ET&D, and incentive systems is a supply-driven ET&D system, where programs are offered without much regard for the demands of the workforce or customer organizations. Like the DoD, the DoT currently has a largely supply-driven system. It is trying to create a demand-driven system by examining workforce competencies and needs and encouraging OAs to use this information in developing learning and development activities. The DoT human resources office produced a conceptual framework intended to link employee development to workforce planning and performance results. The Federal Highway Administration's Professional Capacity Building program was an effort to develop a fundamental knowledge of the competencies it needs for present and future workers. It asked 200 employees in planning, designing, and operating functions about the skills they need to do their jobs. On the private sector side, FIRSCo emphasizes regular and rapid technological advance in the financial industry as a reason to retrain junior and senior employees.

Use Education to Compensate for Recruiting Difficulties

As noted above, the DoD civilian workforce (and the federal civilian workforce in general) is aging. Baby boomers are nearing retirement, and competition from the private sector hinders efforts to attract new hires. Although addressing this challenge is not a responsibility of the Chancellor's office, there are ways that the office could promote the use of ET&D as a powerful workforce-shaping tool.

The Department of Transportation shares many workforce characteristics with the DoD and recognizes that to attract high-quality employees, agencies have to demonstrate the ability to support their continued learning and development. This is thought of as the Arthur Andersen model—an employee could go virtually anywhere after working there because it is common knowledge that Andersen invests in employee learning. DoT also realizes that it needs to cultivate its existing workforce to compensate for the reduced success in recruiting new personnel. Accordingly, top-level management requires current and future leaders to be identified at all levels of management in the OAs and to attend leadership conferences. A major interest has been linking learning activities with workforce changes and, through the learning activities, ensuring the transfer of human capital needed by rewarding both parties for participating in mentoring activities.

NEXT STEPS

The Chancellor's office faces a truly unique set of challenges and opportunities. No organization we studied parallels the situation of the Chancellor's office well enough to recommend adoption of that organization's entire planning process. As a result, the literature suggests that the instinct in the Chancellor's office to develop a clear sense of identity/purpose is a good one. In our definition, this is the development of a clear vision. That should be the office's next strategic step. The literature on high-performing systems points to the efficacy of a clear vision,[5] and the value of a clear vision in organizations similar to the Chancellor's office was reinforced during at least two of the site visits.

Developing a vision is an idiosyncratic, creative act, little helped by traditional strategic planning processes,[6] but there are at least some criteria by which to measure the suitability of a candidate vision.[7] In the Chancellor's office, this should consist primarily of the selection of an identity/purpose from among the candidates (as augmented above).

Having codified a clear sense of identity/purpose, the next step should be to develop a strategy that will, first and foremost, create a governance structure, keeping in mind the lessons identified in this study. A variety of strategy development techniques exist for this purpose,[8] and a number of organizations are available to help in this arena. RAND will aid the Chancellor's office in drawing upon these resources in its future efforts.

---

[5]See, for example, Setear et al. (1990).

[6]As argued in Mintzberg (1994).

[7]See Setear et al. (1990).

[8]Again, see Mintzberg (1994).

INTERVIEW PROTOCOL

OVERALL PURPOSE

The purpose of the interviews is to understand the vision, mission, strategic plan, and implementation plan of the organization and the approaches used in their development. We also want to understand in a general way how the assessment of academic quality and productivity occurs in the system (state, department, corporation, etc.).

BACKGROUND

Purpose: to understand the role of the organization or system in the education and professional development context and also to discover how the organization thinks about strategic planning.

Q1:   To start, please describe the larger context in which this organization operates and the role the organization plays in that context.

Probe (P)1: Who do you consider to be the primary customers of education and professional development efforts in this organization or system? Do you differentiate between customers within your organization and external customers? Are the bill payers different from the consumers of the services?

P2: Who are the providers of education and professional development? Who pays for the cost of providing this education and professional development? Who delivers the education?

Q2:   To help guide the rest of this interview, please help us under-
      stand how your organization thinks about its future direction.
      Do you think in terms of a vision? A mission statement? A
      strategic plan? All of these?

[Note that some flexibility will be needed in the execution of the rest
of the protocol depending on the answer to this question.]

[CHOOSE THE HIGHEST STRATEGIC LEVEL SPECIFIED BY THE
INTERVIEWEE AND SPECIFY THAT THE QUESTIONS THAT YOU
WILL ASK NEXT ADDRESS THAT LEVEL.]

NATURE OF THE ENTERPRISE

Purpose: to learn about the *vision* or mission statement of the organization as a whole and of the education-related sub-unit, if relevant,
and to understand the role of the interviewee in the development
and/or review of the vision.

Q3:   What is the strategic vision, or mission of this organization as a
      whole?

[ASK Q4 IF ONLY A SUBSET OF THE ORGANIZATION HANDLES
THE EDUCATIONAL/PROFESSIONAL DEVELOPMENT FUNC-
TIONS.]

Q4:   Please describe the strategic vision and mission of the educa-
      tion and professional-development-related subset of the or-
      ganization.

Q5:   What are the education and professional-development-related
      mission and responsibilities of this office/position?

[If necessary, say: From this point forward, all the questions I ask will
refer to only the subset of the organization that deals with education
and professional development.]

Q6:   When was the vision/mission statement for education and
      professional development first articulated?

      P: What motivated the organization to articulate a mission
      statement? Was it mandated? Were there environmental pres-
      sures? Trends for the future?

Q7:   Who was involved in the development of this vision?

P1: Were you involved? (If not, ask who was in charge of vision development.)

P2: Was the process limited to only a few key people, or was input provided by different groups within the organization? Please explain.

P3: Was the process documented? If so, where? Can we get access to the documents?

Q8:   What was the process you used to come up with the vision/mission? What considerations guided its development?

P1: Did you have any conceptions about what characteristics a good vision should have? Please explain.

P2: Was the vision or mission statement modeled after those of other organizations, other parts of the same organization, or other sources?

Q9:   Has the vision been re-evaluated since it was first articulated?

P1: When, or how often?

P2: Who participates in the re-evaluation process? Do you?

P3: Please describe the process for re-evaluating the vision and how it differs, if at all, from the initial visioning process.

Q10:   How is the vision communicated to the staff?

P: If I stopped a member of your organization's staff in the halls, do you think he or she would probably be able to articulate the mission of the organization or not?

DEVELOPMENT OF THE STRATEGIC PLAN

Purpose: to understand how the strategic plan was developed and to determine the nature of the plan (i.e., strategic planning or strategic programming); also to learn how priorities are set in the plan.

Q11:   Were the development of a mission statement and the development of the strategic plan part of a single effort, or were they handled separately?

P1: What motivated the development of a strategic plan?

P2: In what ways did the strategic planning process differ from the visioning process?

Q12: Please summarize the main components of the current strategic plan, and in general, how the plan has evolved over time.

P1: How often is the strategic plan reviewed, and who is involved in the review process?

P2: Was the strategic planning process documented? Can we get access to it?

Q13: To the extent that there are multiple goals and objectives in the plan, are there processes for setting priorities among the different components?

P1: Please describe those processes briefly and explain how they factor into the strategic planning process.

P2: Are these processes linked to the mission/vision? If so, how?

Q14: Are the goals and priorities of the strategic plan articulated clearly to all customers?

P1: Are you confident that the goals address the needs of all customers?

[If necessary, ask the following question:]

P2: In the plan, how much importance is placed on investments in employee continuous learning?

IMPLEMENTATION AND GOVERNANCE

Purpose: to understand the governance structure and the mechanisms in place that are implicitly or explicitly assumed to be required for the successful implementation of the strategic plan.

Q15: In what way has implementation of the plan affected people in the system? Does it represent significant changes from the past, or just minor adjustments? Please explain.

Q16:   How is the strategic plan implemented?

P1: Are there *incentive structures* designed to induce components of the organization to follow the strategic plan? If so, who are the targets of these incentive structures? What incentives are used? Can you provide us with an example of such an incentive structure?

P2: Are there *mandates* requiring that components of the organization follow certain steps or programs? If so, are these written down? Is the performance of these components monitored? How much flexibility do the components have to disregard the mandates?

P3: Do the components of this organization face *incentives or mandates from other sources that may conflict* with those designed to promote the strategic plan? If so, what are the sources?

[OFFER CONCRETE EXAMPLES, IF POSSIBLE.]

Q17:   Who makes the implementation decisions?

P: Are budgeting decisions made separately? By whom? How?

EVALUATION OF ORGANIZATIONAL PERFORMANCE

Purpose: to develop a general sense of the criteria used to evaluate the effectiveness of the strategic plan and to determine the mechanisms by which the evaluation affects future strategic planning efforts.

Q18:   Does the strategic planning approach include or propose evaluation criteria that would be used to assess organizational performance relative to the strategic plan? Please explain.

P1: Is comparative evaluation used to set priorities for funding?

P2: Do you use these criteria to assess whether important functions (programs, centers, institutions) are congruent with the overall mission of the organization?

Q19:   What kind of information and/or information systems are provided or proposed to serve the evaluation criteria?

P1: Does the information system rely only on existing data or does it require the collection of additional data?

P2: What kinds of challenges have presented themselves in this area, if any (cost, availability, etc.)?

Q20: When and how is the success of the strategic plan ultimately evaluated?

Q21: In view of the mission, are you aware of any shortcomings in the evaluation criteria? Please explain.

CLOSING QUESTION FOR STRATEGIC PLANNING SECTION

Q22: Stepping back now, and considering all that we've discussed today, in your opinion, what is working well and badly in the design and implementation of the strategic plan? Please explain.

OVERVIEW OF QUALITY AND PRODUCTIVITY ASSESSMENT EFFORTS

Purpose: to obtain an overview of quality and productivity assessment efforts, including any documentation that might be available.

Q23: Do you have an explicit program for evaluating the quality and productivity of education and professional development activities? If so, please describe the effort.

Q24: Is assessment linked to other efforts (state accountability, strategic planning, budget processes, other types of higher education reform)?

Q25: Is participation in assessment voluntary on the part of sub-units of your organization?

Q26: How often are institutions or programs assessed?

Q27: What is the total cost of the assessment and who pays?

Q28: Is the quality and productivity assessment program documented? Is there any documentation we could obtain from you?

Measuring and Evaluating Quality and Productivity

Purpose: to determine whether and how the assessment process identifies the outcomes of interest and creates appropriate measures of academic quality and productivity. Also to determine the way in which performance measures are used to evaluate success or failure.

Q29: What measures do you use to evaluate quality and productivity?

Q30: Are there objective standards against which the performance measures are compared?

Perspectives on the Value of the Current System

Q31: What happens with the results of the evaluation?

P1: Is funding affected?

P2: Are programs eliminated or institutions closed down?

Q32: How would you rate the current system?

Q33: Those are all the questions we have for you today. Thanks very much for your time. Are there any questions you have for us?

CASE STUDIES FROM THE LITERATURE

Appendix B contains detailed case studies from the literature. To select the cases, we relied on expert opinion, both published and unpublished. We contacted experts within each category of organization identified in Chapter Five as potentially similar to the Chancellor's office and asked the experts to identify the institution or institutions exhibiting best practices in strategic and performance planning within that category. We then looked for consensus among the various published opinions and verbal responses. Where we found consensus, we performed a case study. Accordingly, for some categories only one case study was performed; for others, we performed several.

WESTERN ASSOCIATION OF SCHOOLS AND COLLEGES

Background

WASC is one of the regional accrediting associations in the United States. It evaluates and accredits schools, colleges, and universities in California, Hawaii, American Samoa, Guam, the Commonwealth of the Northern Marianas, the Republic of the Marshall Islands, the Federated States of Micronesia, and the Republic of Palau. WASC currently serves 146 accredited and candidate institutions throughout its region. It functions through a board of directors and three accrediting commissions: the Accrediting Commission for Senior Colleges and Universities, the Accrediting Commission for Community and Junior Colleges, and the Accrediting Commission for Schools. The board of directors consists of nine members; each accrediting commission selects three members to serve on the board. This appendix focuses on the efforts of the Accrediting Commission for Senior Colleges and Universities.

As with the other accrediting agencies, WASC's power is based in the power of accreditation itself. WASC has the power to deny accreditation or make accreditation contingent on the school's meeting certain standards. Colleges and universities that want to be accredited strive to comply with the rules and regulations established by WASC and the other accrediting agencies. The following are some of the reasons that institutions pursue accreditation:

- The stamp of approval from accrediting agencies enables student consumers to know that the institution or program meets a minimal set of criteria.

- The process offers education providers evidence for determining whether to accept or recognize credit for courses taken outside their institution.

- The federal government uses accreditation status to determine an institution's eligibility for federal student financial aid. It awards federal financial aid only to students enrolled at accredited institutions or at institutions that are candidates for accreditation.

- Most professional societies will license students only if they have completed their studies at an accredited institution.

Nature of the Enterprise

The purpose of WASC is to foster the continual improvement of education and cooperation among educational institutions and agencies, the certification of accreditation or candidacy status, and the promotion of effective working relationships with other educational organizations and accrediting agencies. The primary purpose of all commission activities is to strengthen institutions through self-study, peer evaluation, and appropriate follow-up. The commission seeks to sustain the quality and integrity of institutions. During review, a college is judged by how effectively it meets its stated mission and WASC standards.[1]

Development of the Strategic Plan

In considering its purpose and practices during the early 1990s, WASC leadership saw a disparity between the accreditation process and the accreditors' goals. Two major commission task forces began work in 1994–95 and ultimately called for more flexible approaches to accreditation as well as for increased attention to both assessment of the effectiveness of the educational programs of institutions and to demonstrated student learning. This work led to several retreats in 1996 and 1997 focused on reviewing internal and external factors affecting accreditation. WASC staff felt that as accreditors they needed to better understand the student context (e.g., students taking courses at multiple institutions or transferring from a community college to an institution that grants bachelor's degrees). In addition, multimodal (distance and site-based) delivery now exists at institutions and was not reflected in the accreditation process.

WASC invited leading thinkers in educational effectiveness to write concept papers to develop a clearer definition of what an accreditation process organized around these ideas might look like. In addition, it hosted small group sessions with Accreditation Liaison Officers to discuss different aspects of restructuring the accreditation process.

As a result, WASC is now redesigning its Standards of Accreditation and the policies and procedures in its *Handbook of Accreditation.* The agency has posed a series of questions to guide its planning process and consideration of its future role: What would an "effectiveness centered" process look like, for the institution as well as for a team? What would the commission's role be? How would student work be used? How would we look at raw data, institutional systems, or recommendations for change? The principles guiding the planning process are outlined in WASC (1998).

---

[1]See the WASC website for the most current version of the standards, at http://www.wascweb.org/senior/handbook/standards.pdf.

To share lessons learned during its strategic planning process, WASC published a resource manual on assessment in 1992 but feels a continuing need to create a library of relevant documents addressing student learning and assessment. WASC plans to provide these resources in both hard copy and web-based format.

Implementation and Governance

In the past, WASC's accreditation procedures have focused on the existence of institutional structures and processes, such as whether the institution has a mission statement, planning processes, faculty senate, and program review procedures. In the future, it plans to place more emphasis on the effectiveness of these processes and how they affect student learning.

A significant number of institutions in WASC's region have been open to and interested in putting greater emphasis on student learning and have taken steps in this direction. The opportunity is available for institutions to work collaboratively with WASC to develop better practices, to use the self-study process to focus on educational effectiveness and student learning, and to have the review team provide feedback and counsel on how to improve. WASC is aware that during this experimental period some approaches will be successful and others will not, and it plans to publicize both the successes and failures.

As part of this restructuring, WASC plans more effective use of data that campuses already collect and may shift to data portfolios that reflect the institution's core competencies. Currently, the accreditation process requires that institutions collect data solely for the purposes of accreditation and such data collection does not always help the institution in its own self-assessment.

The Invitation to Dialogue process was intended to serve as a check on WASC's accreditation approach, and in this way, WASC's stakeholders were able to assess WASC's work. In addition, WASC has an evaluation committee whose purpose is to assess the work of the commission itself. As WASC continues with the planning process, the evaluation committee will use surveys and other instruments to en-sure that the agency stays connected to regional issues.

Discussion

WASC has put tremendous thought and effort into reconsidering and rewriting its standards and review process. Because the goal was to make the accreditation process more reflective of institutional mis-sion and purpose, the agency solicited a great deal of input from a wide range of stakeholders. In addition, WASC leadership is working with a number of schools to test different approaches and work out difficulties before imposing a new system on a large number of insti-tutions. WASC hopes that this flexible, iterative approach will lead to a process that institutions find more relevant and helpful than the current system.

FIRSCO'S SERVICE DELIVERY UNIVERSITY

Background

FIRSCo, a division of Fidelity, had undergone an unprecedented pe-riod of growth in the early 1990s when it made the decision in 1993 to build a corporate university. Its client base and assets under man-agement were increasing at a rate of 40 percent per year, and it was also expanding into new markets with new products. That same growth, however, required that FIRSCo add upward of ten people per week to its staff of 1,400. In the rapidly changing world of financial services, FIRSCo became concerned that its competitiveness would be limited both by the relative lack of experience of its junior work-force and by the inability of even more-seasoned employees to keep up with the state of the art. The best response to challenges stem-ming from rapid growth and continuous change, top management believed, was to create a model of employee development. The re-sult was SDU.

Today, FIRSCo manages corporate retirement 401(k) plans for more than 5,700 organizations representing nearly four million individual participants. Each of its employees (termed "associates") receives 80 hours of developmental activity per year through SDU.

Nature of the Enterprise

SDU aligns all training and education with FIRSCo's major business objectives:

- Set the industry standard in customer service.
- Sustain double-digit annual growth.
- Continue to achieve profitability in all segments of the business.

Every class, through its case studies, reading materials, and discussions, addresses these goals and the best ways to achieve them. SDU envisions the service-profit chain as one that begins with employee satisfaction and loyalty: loyal, satisfied employees drive customer satisfaction and loyalty, which in turn drive profit and growth.

Development of the Strategic Plan

SDU's highest priorities were set at the time of its founding and are clearly aligned with FIRSCo's major business goals. They are to engender associates who regard service delivery "as a discipline with its own skills, competencies, and vocabulary" (i.e., those who understand service as a business) and to create an organization in which "every individual can and should make decisions that deliver solutions to customers."

Management buy-in to the strategic aims for FIRSCo's corporate university is promoted by giving line managers themselves a strong voice in SDU governance (through deanships and advisory board memberships as well as through teaching responsibilities). A second incentive is generated by linking a percentage of every manager's bonus to the manager's performance in completing professional development plans with employees and ensuring their fulfillment.

Relatively junior associates as well as managers comparatively new to that role were "hungry for education and training." They needed no special incentives; for them SDU filled an immediate need.

Implementation and Governance

A number of factors helped to drive the implementation of SDU. As explained above, two key influences from the outset were the need to respond effectively to rapid growth and the need to adapt to continuous technical change in the financial services industry.

To achieve these aims through a corps of learning-oriented service professionals, SDU established a foundation, or core curriculum, that would provide technical, regulatory, and industry information to associates so that they could perform basic financial service functions competently.

Foundation courses are generally short, content-based, and practical. SDU also comprises five colleges that offer courses requiring higher levels of cognitive learning; each college offers a range of courses organized under a goal that serves the priorities noted above. Their roles are summarized below:

- The Customer Service College aims to create a company-wide dialogue about service excellence and how it is best delivered.

- The Operations Management College relates the practices, procedures, and principles of running a big business to service delivery.

- The Risk Management College is designed to create a company-wide awareness of risk; to develop an ability to identify, analyze, and manage risk; and to determine how to build internal risk controls.

- The Sales and Marketing College teaches associates how FIRSCo positions itself in the marketplace; how to improve relationships with clients; and how to stay market-focused, flexible, and responsive.

- The Leadership and Management Development College aims to reinforce a leadership culture built on management's belief that everyone in the company needs to embrace responsibility for the business.

Underlying SDU is the assumption that the primary responsibility for professional development should rest with line managers (rather than the Learning and Development (L&D) Department, as FIRSCo's human resources department is called).

SDU is headed by a chancellor who is a line manager. The five colleges that constitute SDU are headed by deans, each of whom is also a line manager. The colleges are assisted by advisory boards whose members help shape the curriculum and course content. These advisors, along with the teaching faculty, are managers as well. Finally, all of FIRSCo's managers are responsible for working with the associates who report to them to design personalized development plans and to make sure the plans are fulfilled (see Development of the Strategic Plan, above).

Two key purposes are served by the intensive involvement of managers in SDU. First, it sends a message to associates and to managers that FIRSCo is serious about its commitment to development. Second, it is the line managers who know the business best—so they are in the best position to connect learning to business performance goals.

The L&D Department works as a partner with SDU in performing the following functions. It looks across the organization as a whole, assessing gaps in skills and recommending curriculum solutions to address them. Second, it brings its expertise in training and education to bear on the design of instructional materials and pedagogical approaches. Third, it is responsible for developing and administering SDU's core courses. Finally, it handles administration—finding rooms, scheduling classes, buying case study materials, and gathering feedback on courses and programs.

Evaluation of Organizational Performance

Even before launching SDU, FIRSCo realized that it would be difficult to measure the university's success. The performance improvement aims for SDU are inextricably tied to FIRSCo business objectives, and the latter are measurable. Moreover, those performance indicators have shown positive change. For instance, improved development for associates was expected to improve customer satisfaction levels and to reduce operating losses. Both outcomes have been realized since the inception of SDU. However, there is no way to establish a direct causal link between these outcomes and the professional development provided by SDU because so many other variables also affect service quality. On the other hand, data are collected that establish inferential links between such outcomes and education/training experiences (see below).

Several types of data are collected to assess SDU's efforts. They include the following:

- L&D regularly reassesses the match between knowledge and skill needs in FIRSCo's business lines and the courses offered by SDU.

- Employee self-evaluations are gathered on a pre/post basis; these assessments include employees' perceptions of their own effect on the customers' satisfaction.

- Reduction in time to perform key tasks is regularly measured (e.g., amount of elapsed time from start of work on a new customer plan until the plan "goes live" (becomes official and active) or reduction in the turnaround time for customer problem resolution).

- Improved cognitive performance is measured by reduction in the frequency with which supervisors must be consulted in the course of resolving customer problems.

Besides such formal measures, a growing collection of anecdotes illustrates development-based performance improvements. Says SDU's chancellor, "Will we ever be able to measure the financial impact of [an] employee's training at SDU? The answer is no. Does that mean we should not have made the investment until we had a perfect measurement system? Not at all."

Discussion

FIRSCo's development of SDU as a key component of its successful overall strategy incorporates a number of potentially generalizeable points. They are highlighted briefly here.

- Major changes in the broader environment (in this case, work-force demographics plus the nature of the financial services sector) would soon present serious business problems for FIRSCo; its future success was likely to depend on continuous development of its pool of human resources.

- Although provision of high-quality professional education and training was a logical response to the impending challenge, selling it as a high priority throughout the corporation was seen as necessary for moving from stated visions to effective actions.

- Critical steps to successful implementation included directly linking professional education and training not only to the corporation's business objectives but also to every line manager's annual performance reviews.

Perhaps most important, FIRSCO's SDU story is not one that depends for its success on a single charismatic leader or a sink-or-swim crisis to effect change. Rather it illustrates an astute and well-designed application of organizational change theory to reach its goals.

BACKGROUND ON FEDERAL AGENCIES

With the passage of GPRA in 1993, federal agencies are now required to submit five-year strategic plans as well as annual performance plans alongside their budget requests to Congress. Progress toward fulfilling these requirements has been slow, as agencies struggle to articulate and define both their mission and the appropriate organizational performance measurement indicators. The GAO and the OMB have been providing feedback and guidance to agencies since the bill's inception, and various congressional committees have also been actively involved in overseeing its implementation. The consensus among these three stakeholders is that, among the federal agency strategic plans submitted, the Department of Education, Social Security Administration, and the Department of Transportation have all created the most successful strategic plans according to the specified dimensions of GPRA.

DEPARTMENT OF EDUCATION

Nature of the Enterprise

The Department of Education's mission statement is "to ensure equal access to education and to promote educational excellence throughout the nation."[2]

Development of Strategic Plan

Drafts of the plan were circulated throughout the department and meetings were held by assistant secretaries to elicit feedback, ideas for improvement, and strategies for implementation. Congress, the GAO, and other stakeholders, such as state and local governments, school districts, postsecondary institutions, and education, community, civil rights, and business organizations interested in education, were consulted.

Implementation and Governance

At the highest level, resource allocation authority and responsibility lie with Congress and the legislation it passes in support of department initiatives and programs.

"Objective leaders" will be designated to oversee the accomplishment of specific objectives and will report on progress to the deputy secretary and senior officials. Staff and program offices will review progress on individual program performance plans.

The plan is being implemented in response to the GPRA. The Annual Performance Plan is required by law to be sent to Congress along with the department's budget request. Ultimately, Congress deems the strategic plan a success or failure.

Evaluation of Organizational Performance

Each overall strategic goal has a list of performance indicators that will be used to assess progress in the Annual Performance Plan.

---

[2]Department of Education (1997).

The individual program performance plans for the 90 activity areas will be aligned with the strategic plan in the Annual Performance Plan.

Program evaluations, assessments conducted by the department and other federal agencies, statistical studies, and grantee performance data systems will provide the necessary information to measure progress on the performance indicators. Most of the data collection efforts are already in place, but in some cases they will be refined to align more closely with the performance indicators.

SOCIAL SECURITY ADMINISTRATION

Nature of the Enterprise

The Social Security Administration's mission is "to promote the economic security of the nation's people through compassionate and vigilant leadership in shaping and managing America's social security programs."[3]

Development of Strategic Plan

The Social Security Administration consulted many stakeholders, including employees, Congress, the GAO, the OMB, interest groups, unions and management associations, other federal agencies, and SSA's advisory board to elicit feedback on drafts of the plan.

Implementation and Governance

The decisionmaking authority and responsibility lie with a centralized policymaking and administrative staff who support the national network of 1,500 regional offices.

At the highest level, resource allocation authority and responsibility lie with Congress and the legislation it passes in support of department initiatives and programs.

---

[3]Social Security Administration (1997).

The plan is being implemented in response to the GPRA. The Annual Performance Plan is required by law to be sent to Congress along with the department's budget request. Ultimately, Congress deems the strategic plan a success or failure.

Evaluation of Organizational Performance

"Program evaluation is used continuously at SSA as a tool for setting goals, defining strategies, initiating change and determining success" (SSA (1997), Section IV). Each agency goal includes specific performance indicators that will be used to assess progress.

A requirement laid out in the agency strategic plan is that a cost-benefit analysis be conducted for every major SSA initiative, "on all effects, operational, internal and external, administrative, and program-related," to help make the optimal choices about where to direct resources (SSA (1997), Section IV).

Existing data collection systems will be augmented with "new measures and measurement systems established to support the GPRA focus on program outcomes; systems will be designed to ensure that the information they collect will not only reflect performance but drive corrective action" (SSA (1997), Section IV).

UNIVERSITY SYSTEM OF GEORGIA

Background

The University System of Georgia was created in 1931 and consists of four universities, two regional universities, 13 state universities, and 15 associate degree colleges. The system is governed, controlled, and managed by a board of regents appointed by the governor. The board has 16 members, five from the state at large and one each from the 11 congressional districts. The board elects a chancellor to be its chief executive officer and the chief administrative officer of the university system.

The charter for what is now the University of Georgia (which was the first higher education institution in the state) was granted in 1785. The number of campuses in the state gradually increased over time and in 1929 that state expressed interest in creating a central governing board. In August 1931, the Board of Regents for the University System of Georgia was established through the Reorganization Act. The board originally consisted of 11 members (one from each congressional district and one at-large). The act was designed to address fears that the various institutions were competing for resources and by acting independently were not serving the interests of the state as a whole.

In its early years the board consolidated a number of campuses. Then, the system came under attack in 1943, which led to the Southern Association of Colleges and Schools (SACS) (the regional accrediting agency) withdrawing accreditation from ten institutions. SACS identified problems with irregularities and outside interference into academic activities. To free the board from outside influences, the governor made the board a constitutional body.

The principles set forth in the 1932 act continue to guide the state's higher education system (and were included in the new state constitution that was approved in 1982). The board's powers include: "authority for program approval or discontinuance, internal allocation of the budget, facilities construction, and decisions concerning adding new initiatives, upgrading or downgrading the level of an institution, or closure or merger of institutions."[4]

Nature of the Enterprise

The board of regents for the University System of Georgia spelled out its vision for the system in *Access to Academic Excellence for the New Millennium*. It saw its role as promoting "the continuing improvement of every unit and of the System as a coordinated whole." The vision, developed by the board in 1994, was intended to guide long-term planning and decisionmaking and it still continues to shape the board's work today.

> As Georgia emerges as a leader in a global society, the university system of Georgia will lead in access to academic excellence. Among the nation's public universities and colleges, Georgia's will be recognized for first-rate undergraduate education, leading-edge

---

[4]See http://www.peachnet.edu/admin/pubs/infodig/infodig97/history.html.

research, and committed public service. Georgians will appreciate the system's prestige and leadership in public higher education, including its graduate and professional programs, as fundamental to the state's economic, social, technological, and cultural advancement. The university system of Georgia and its component colleges and universities will sustain close contact with the people of Georgia, be responsive to the needs of Georgians first and foremost while raising their aspirations, and generate a more highly educated populace throughout the state. It will seek to create for students from various backgrounds every possible avenue to intellectual achievement without compromising academic excellence and challenge them to their full potential for leadership. Its students, who are its heart and soul, will therefore be its strongest supporters (The University System of Georgia, n.d.).

Development of the Strategic Plan

In addition to the millennium document, the board of regents approved the *University System of Georgia Comprehensive Plan 1996–97*, which was put together by the strategic planning committee of the board of regents (Board of Regents, 1997). The board first adopted the planning assumptions (December 1996), and then developed and approved planning principles in each of four areas: enrollment planning (December 1996), workforce development (February 1997), academic program development (April 1997), and capital planning (May 1997). The board also approved planning results and actions for each area. The planning assumptions relate to Georgia's demography and economic resources, the university system's role in Georgia, enrollment demand, workforce demand, delivering instruction, and linking planning, facilities, and budgeting.

Not only does the system have the millennium document and comprehensive plan, but it also has 34 "Guiding Principles for Strategic Action." These principles are divided into multiple categories,[5] the first of which is not titled and addresses overarching themes. As an example, the first principle is:

---

[5]See http://www.peachnet.edu/admin/pubs/infodig/infodig97/guide.html.

- Shall stimulate Georgians' aspirations for higher education, have high academic standards for its students and programs, challenge and assist students to meet or exceed those standards, provide sound academic and career advice, help students prepare for employment and lifelong education in a changing world, and increase the number of well educated Georgians.

The remaining principles fall into the categories of academic excellence and recognition, development of human resources, efficient use of resources, system strength through governance, and effective external partnerships. An example of academic excellence is:

- Shall promote to Georgians and the nation its commitment to service by supporting strong undergraduate, graduate, and professional education; path-breaking research and creativity; and other national patterns of academic excellence in its curricula and operations.

The first of the principles addressing development of human resources says:

- Shall recruit aggressively and nationally for talented, diverse faculty to serve the various missions of its institutions. It shall also develop and retain faculty in an attractive, collaborative, productive environment for teaching and learning that includes, for both non-tenured and tenured faculty: clear personnel standards and policies; expectations and programs for continued professional growth; resources to support excellence in teaching, scholarship, research, and community service; competitive compensation and other recognition for meritorious performance.

The leading principle relating to efficient use of resources says:

- Shall have strategic enrollment policies that determine the number of students its various institutions can serve excellently based on its projected resources. It shall forecast changes in student demand and resources, prepare effectively for those changes, market the full range of its campus settings, and make optimal use of all existing human and physical resources, including the access-cornerstone capabilities of its two-year colleges, to advance Georgians' access to academic quality.

In terms of effective external partnerships, the system:

- Shall create deep, rich partnerships with elementary and secondary schools by initiating supporting collaborative faculty development, dynamic and sustained pre-college programs, and other projects throughout its institutions to assist in insuring that Georgia's children and young people receive strong preparation and advisement for college study and lifelong learning.

Implementation and Governance

Four of the 34 "Guiding Principles for Strategic Action" directly address governance:

- Shall maximize the effectiveness of its Board of Regents in setting policy and priorities, communicating its will on a continuing basis through a well staffed Chancellor's office, and guiding toward its vision the System's institutions and program operations through the presidents.

- Shall exercise the Board of Regents' constitutional governance authority over its institutions within the context of constructive, continuous relationships with the General Assembly, the Governor's office, and other state agencies.

- Shall use the best management practices of continuous strategic planning and quality improvement, suitable standards and rewards, and regular assessment reviews, and a focus on learning productivity, all in an atmosphere of cooperation and accountability. It shall thereby insure the implementation of its policies, the effectiveness of its programs and units and administrative leaders, and proper stewardship by its Board of state resources to provide Georgians access to Academic excellence.

- Shall develop reliable, broad-based data and draw on effective advice—including state, regional, and institutional perspectives of administration, faculty, students, community leaders, and other stakeholders—for its policy decisions.

Campuses have some discretion over implementation of the principles, although the system's planning priorities must be reflected in the institutions' strategic plans, and state directives relate to the implementation of some of the principles. For example, one principle is that "each institution has a clear, substantive, distinctive mission." The specific directives to implement that principle are, for the Chancellor's office:

- written documents detailing other system-wide parameters for developing institutional missions, including specific questions to be addressed and report format; guidelines and processes for developing missions in relationship to ongoing institutional strategic planning.

For institutions:

- (1) How its proposed mission statement supports the institution's current range and scope of academic programs, its distinctive strengths, and its relationship to other University System and nearby institutions. And, (2) how it supports the institution's vision for its future within the System's strategic planning environment, including any new program requests and discontinuations anticipated over the next 5–7 years. A preliminary one-page, well-reasoned, data-based justification for any anticipated new program request should be included.

Evaluation of Organizational Performance

Data related to several of the principles are listed in the planning document. Enrollment targets are identified for each campus—the targets are for each year of the five-year planning period; a range of between –2 percent and +2 percent is also identified to help keep campuses on track. Workforce data are also documented, with the unmet need of numerous occupations listed in the report. In addition, the report lists the costs of major capital priorities for each institution in the system.

Discussion

The University System of Georgia, like the other state-level systems, has worked hard to balance the interests of individual campuses with the goals of the state as a whole. At the same time, the state's higher education planners have attempted to create a dynamic; they want the system and institutions to be able to react to changes in the state's demographics and economy. Finally, a key step that the system has taken to improve planning is to link planning with assessment and budgeting, so that each informs the other.

CALIFORNIA STATE UNIVERSITY

Background

The CSU is one of three public higher education systems in California (along with the University of California (UC) and the community colleges). The CSU system consists of 23 comprehensive universities located throughout the state and accepts the top third of entering college students (the UC schools accept the top 12 percent and the community colleges accept all students). The major roles and responsibilities of the system were spelled out in the 1960 California Master Plan (described in more detail below; see also Master Plan Survey Team (1960)).

Responsibility for the California State University is vested in the board of trustees, whose members are appointed by the state governor. The trustees appoint the chancellor, the chief executive officer of the system, and the presidents—the chief executive officers of the respective campuses. The trustees, the chancellor, and the presidents develop systemwide policy, with actual implementation at the campus level taking place through broadly based consultative procedures. The Academic Senate of the California State University, made up of elected representatives of the faculty from each campus, recommends academic policy to the board of trustees through the chancellor.

The CSU system engaged in a strategic planning process between 1996 and 1998, culminating in the *Cornerstones Report* (CSU, 1997). At the time, the state faced two major crises: a crisis of funding and resources, exaggerated by growing enrollment demand in the state, and the state's ongoing social, demographic, and economic changes (namely, growing diversity).

Nature of the Enterprise

The mission of the California State University encompasses the following:

- To advance and extend knowledge, learning, and culture, especially throughout California.

- To provide opportunities for individuals to develop intellectually, personally, and professionally.

- To prepare significant numbers of educated, responsible people to contribute to California's schools, economy, culture, and future.

- To encourage and provide access to an excellent education to all who are prepared for and wish to participate in collegiate study.

- To offer undergraduate and graduate instruction leading to bachelor's and higher degrees in the liberal arts and sciences, the applied fields, and the professions, including the doctoral degree when authorized.

- To prepare students for an international, multicultural society.

- To provide public services that enrich the university and its communities.

Development of the Strategic Plan

In 1997, the Office of the CSU Chancellor completed the Cornerstones planning process and report, which is intended to guide the CSU into the next century. It delineates ten guiding principles as well as recommendations on how to implement those principles. Cornerstones attempts to strike a balance between the responsibilities of the individual campuses in relation to the Chancellor's office. Significantly, the Cornerstones development process was not designed to be a comprehensive institutional planning process; it took as given the goals, mission, and policies for the CSU that are spelled out in *The California State Master Plan for Higher Education*.[6]

---

[6]Select Committee on the Master Plan (1972).

The Cornerstones group consisted of 24 members, including trustees, faculty, students, presidents, and senior system administrators. Four task forces each addressed one of the "cornerstones" of the CSU: (1) learning for the 21st century; (2) meeting the enrollment and resource challenge; (3) institutional integrity, performance, and accountability; and (4) post-baccalaureate and continuing education. Following completion of draft reports, forums and meetings were held on the campuses to provide feedback on the individual reports as well as the Cornerstones principles document. Revisions were made based on the feedback received, and another round of consultations and revisions followed. Ultimately, the board approved the final report.

As noted, Cornerstones took as given the goals, mission, and policies for CSU detailed in the California Master Plan. The four areas addressed by the policy goals in the Master Plan are educational results, ensuring access, financial stability, and ensuring accountability. The recommendations for educational results suggest operational, organizational, and programmatic changes. The goal of ensuring access will be achieved through outreach and retention, support for K–12 (to better prepare students coming into the system), and stronger relationships with community colleges (because many CSU students transfer from community colleges). Financial stability will be a shared responsibility between the state and the CSU system. CSU will work with the state to ensure adequate funding and will work within its own institutions to increase productivity across numerous dimensions. Finally, the CSU system will ensure accountability both as a system serving the needs of the state and as a collection of autonomous, diverse, individual campuses.

Implementation and Governance

Cornerstones is an umbrella effort, informed by and in many cases building on existing campus efforts. For most of the initiatives, the individual campuses will have flexibility in implementation of the principles. For the remaining few, the Chancellor's office is calling for a standard approach for implementation across campuses—with regard to the access goals in particular. In the implementation document, priorities are listed as either "system priority," "campus priority," or "system and campus priority."

Cornerstones clearly spells out the priorities for the institutions, and the *Cornerstones Implementation Plan* (CSU, 1998) outlines specific steps that faculty and staff at the individual universities can take to achieve the principles in the *Cornerstones Report.*

Evaluation of Organizational Performance

To measure progress toward the goals spelled out in Cornerstones, institutions are being asked to collect various data. Specifically, the implementation plan makes some general statements about data that should be collected to support particular principles. For example, to support Principle 1 (what students need to learn and know to graduate): "Each university will periodically collect, analyze, and evaluate evidence of the extent to which its students are achieving the learning outcomes to which it is publicly committed." Similar statements are made for the other nine guiding principles.[7]

Discussion

In designing Cornerstones, planners were very cognizant of the role of the individual campuses within the CSU system, and the CSU system in relation to the state's three-part system of public colleges and universities. For that reason, the developers tried to build on campus initiatives and listed items as being either a "system priority," "campus priority," or "system and campus priority." In this way, the planners made an effort to balance responsibilities between the campuses and the Chancellor's office.

THE CALIFORNIA MASTER PLAN

Background

California policymakers have been interested in the development of higher education in the state since the early 1900s. As early as 1899, a commission was formed to study the state's educational system. The state is best known however, for the 1960 passage of the *Master Plan*

---

[7]See the CSU website, at http://www.calstate.edu/cornerstones/reports/implment.html.

for Higher Education in California. In 1957, California, under the direction of the State Board of Education, conducted several studies that laid the groundwork for the Master Plan. A liaison committee representing the State Board of Education and the Regents of the University of California completed *A Study of the Need for Additional Centers of Public Higher Education in California* (Joint Staff for the Committee, 1957). The committee had two charges:

- To develop a priority list for areas of the state now inadequately served by junior colleges, state colleges, and campuses of the University of California.

- To show the effect which the establishment of new institutions would have on existing ones.

In addition, its research was guided by two principles set out by the board and the regents:

- The expansion of existing institutions and the establishment of new ones should depend on the optimum use of the state's resources for higher education in relation to the greatest relative need both geographically and functionally.

- Differentiation of functions so far as possible of the three segments of public higher education, namely, the junior colleges, the state colleges, and the University of California, is imperative if unnecessary and wasteful duplication is to be avoided.

The principles stemmed from the haphazard development in higher education before that point and from the multiple proposals being considered at the state and local level regarding the building of new campuses. A number of legislators and leaders in higher education recognized the need for more thoughtful and systematic planning. At the same time, the three segments had been developing with different missions, and the liaison committee wanted to formalize those differences. The committee concluded that the state urgently needed to expand the number of junior colleges, state colleges, and University of California campuses.

Following the completion of the above described work, the California legislature passed Assembly Concurrent Resolution Number 88 in

1959, which requested that the liaison committee develop a Master Plan for Higher Education.

Nature of the Enterprise

The Master Plan articulated the roles and missions for each segment of California public higher education. As spelled out in the Master Plan, the three segments included the UC system, the CSU system, and the California Community Colleges (CCC, originally called junior colleges). Today, there are nine University of California campuses, 22 CSU campuses, and more than 100 community colleges in operation. In addition, about 150 private institutions operate in the state. The California Postsecondary Education Commission (CPEC) is the statewide coordinating agency that advises the legislature, governor, and postsecondary institutions on higher education issues.

UC admits the top 12 percent of high school students; CSU admits the top one-third, and CCC takes all applicants. UC can offer doctoral and professional graduate education; CSU can offer the teaching credential and other master's degrees; community colleges can offer anything less than a bachelor's degree. The community colleges are the least "system-like" of the three systems, a reflection of the importance of local control for the community colleges.

Development of the Strategic Plan

The Master Plan was the culmination of the work of the liaison committee. The committee's work was motivated by several factors:

- "Large increases in enrollments during the fifties and even larger enrollments projected for the sixties.

- Almost uncontrolled aspirations and proposals of local communities for local public campuses.

- Fear by each segment of higher education of having unbridled competition minimize its potential and role. While state colleges (CSU campuses), formerly known as normal schools, received legislative authority to expand the curricula from the original teacher education, private universities had a large market share and felt threatened by the insensitive expansion of public universities.

- A plethora of proposals to reorganize the structure of the state's systems of higher education.

- A desire in the State Legislature to remove many of the educational questions from the political arena and to provide a system for orderly growth for the sixties and early seventies" (Select Committee on the Master Plan, 1972, p. iii.).

In addition to the Master Plan, a second study was conducted: *Institutional Capacities and Area Needs of California Public Higher Education* (Technical Committee on Institutional Capacities and Area Needs, 1961). This study detailed projections (up to 1975) on enrollment and estimated the need for additional faculty and facilities. At the time, California had 148 colleges and universities catering to some 220,000 students across the state. The study predicted that enrollment would triple by 1975 at all levels of education (bachelor's degree, master's degree, and doctorate). The liaison committee in charge of the study recommended developing new facilities within the UC family and diverting the current flow of students to smaller state colleges to alleviate overcrowding of existing UC campuses. Growth in enrollment would also require hiring additional faculty to maintain low teacher-student ratios.

A third study examined the costs of higher education in California. The study analyzed past cost trends in higher education for the state and recommended cost-saving practices. In addition, the study highlighted current costs for different types of institutions in existence and estimated the costs of expanding existing campuses versus developing new ones. Finally, costs of higher education through 1975 were forecast to increase by more than 20 percent.

The liaison committee had overall responsibility for the process and included ten members from the State Board of Education and the UC regents. It appointed a Master Plan Survey Team of eight members, representing UC, state colleges, community colleges, the state board, K–12 education, and the independent colleges and universities. This group, in turn, drew on numerous advisory groups during the course of its research. The main architects of the Master Plan were Clark Kerr, the president of the University of California at the time; Roy

Simpson, the superintendent of public instruction representing the state colleges; and Arthur Coons, the president of Occidental College (a private institution).

The first set of groups represented the legislature and other state agencies. Technical committees from this group advised the survey team on enrollment projections, selection and retention of students, adult education, the state's ability to finance higher education, the costs of public higher education in California, and institutional capacities and area needs.

Evaluation of Organizational Performance

Numerous studies have been conducted over the years to gauge the effectiveness of California's public higher education system. Some of these have been formal assessments of how the California Master Plan is standing the test of time; others have been studies of particular issues facing higher education and only indirectly look at the effect of the Master Plan. These studies have been conducted by both state-appointed task forces and commissions and by various groups of scholars and researchers. Several examples of these reviews are described below. Most of these efforts have been relatively narrow "topical" studies—rather than comprehensive reviews of the plan. Although it has been reviewed, the plan has not been overhauled in any major way since it was implemented in 1960.

The plan was first reviewed in its entirety in 1965–1966. The reviewers reported on progress in implementation of the 67 recommendations in the Master Plan. They suggested clarifying some of the recommendations, studying others, and dropping one. The reviewers noted changes that occurred between 1960 and 1965 that were not foreseen when the Master Plan was passed (examples include the increasing role of the federal government in financing higher education, the growing strength of state colleges, and the increasing role of faculty in governance).

The most recent formal evaluation took place in 1987 by the Commission for the Review of the Master Plan for Higher Education. These reviewers also outlined several unforeseen problems with the plan and made some recommendations:

- High dropout rates among high school students and inadequate teacher preparation. The plan should include these students through some remedial education at community colleges. UC and CSU campuses should also make a commitment to improve K–12 teacher education, thereby improving the quality of the college population over time.

- The plan expected that customers of the community colleges would always be a youthful and financially able homogeneous population. In truth, the colleges cater to an ethnically diverse population with both part-time and older students.

- Quality of undergraduate education has weakened because of an incentive structure that rewards faculty for research rather than teaching.

- CPEC is weak and unable to offer the unification that the system requires.

Given this set of challenges, the reviewers established four goals for improving the Master Plan. The goals were as follows:

- Unity: clarify the responsibilities of each segment by defining clearer mission statements, guarantee universal access to all undergraduates who qualify, strengthen the governing structure of the community colleges, recognize the California Roundtable[8] as the source of unification.

- Equity: establish new guarantees to have better minority representation, guarantee equity for older students and those requiring financial assistance, hold the board of governors in all segments responsible for retention rates.

- Quality: commit UC and CSU to improving teacher training and research, commit to excellence in teaching among faculty.

- Efficiency: eliminate duplication, contain rising costs.

---

[8]In response to concerns that the three segments operate too independently, the California Roundtable was established in 1979 as a voluntary organization to address issues in higher education.

In 1994, Clark Kerr published an analysis in *Preserving the Master Plan*, in which he outlined a strategy for the future of higher education (Kerr, 1994). He believed that California's recession had brought about competition for resources at a time when needs were expanding. Higher education was competing with health care, public education, welfare, and corrections for funding when enrollments were increasing, older students were returning for more education or retraining, and minorities were increasingly going to college. Kerr considered the lack of consensus for academic decisions and the disconnect between departmental decisions and the offices most closely involved with resource issues as possible roadblocks. He proposed a comprehensive strategy for the subsequent 15 years: focus on a limited range of issues and on resources, involve different levels of leadership in the process, and take action at different levels with respective stakeholders.

In 1997, the California Roundtable was established as a forum for the different stakeholder groups in California higher education. The group, and its advisory board, consisted of representatives from each of the public sector segments, private institutions, and K–12 education and also included other higher education policymakers and experts. The roundtable discussions led to *A Promise Worth Keeping*, which documented the dramatically changed conditions that higher education institutions faced: Tidal Wave II (increasing enrollments), a more ethnically diverse student body, more adult students, and more students not seeking terminal degrees (California Higher Education Policy Center, 1997). The roundtable participants claimed that the funding and reward system were not aligned with the stated objectives of promoting access and that a disconnect existed between the state's objectives and institutional aspirations.

Some of the general criticisms about the higher education system were as follows:

- The current structure is not really one system of higher education. Rather, the three segments offer three distinct systems.

- Governance structures for the three segments are different.

- The current structure does not encourage intersegmental cooperation. In addition, existing collaborations are not tracked by any institution, so no one knows how often collaborations occur.

- Separate parts of the system negotiate independently with the governor and legislature. CPEC is not able to offer the unified voice that the system currently needs.

- Each segment pursues its own interests.

- CPEC offers weak leadership. It has little (if any) influence on the system, in part because many believe that its work is not objective.

Implementation and Governance

The Master Plan clearly laid out the governance structure for each of the three segments as well as the relationship between them. The three segments were intended to constitute one system, but they generally operate independently of one another. In fact, some critics argue that none of the three segments constitutes a single system, let alone the three segments together.

In addition to the three segments with their respective governance structures is the CPEC. CPEC was created in 1974 to be the coordinating board responsible for advising higher education decisionmakers in California. It was intended to be the voice of higher education in the state and its primary responsibilities were as follows:

- Establish a statewide database.

- Review institutional budgets.

- Advise on the need for and location of new campuses.

- Review proposals of new academic programs.

In reality however, CPEC is not particularly powerful. The governor and legislature do not permit the commission to operate freely and CPEC has experienced several budget cuts. In addition, when crucial studies are to be conducted, such as reviewing the Master Plan, the legislature often appoints an independent commission to conduct the work rather than using CPEC. As a result, its most important function is to provide information (e.g., fiscal profiles, student profiles, profiles by theme), even though the commission relies on the three segments for data.

Discussion

The University of California Office of the President website[9] clearly articulates what are considered to be the Master Plan's primary achievements:

- The Master Plan transformed a collection of uncoordinated and competing colleges and universities into a coherent system. It achieved this by assigning each public segment—the University of California, the California State University, and the Community Colleges—its own distinctive mission and pool of students. The genius of the Master Plan was that it established a broad framework for higher education that encourages each of the three public segments to concentrate on creating its own distinctive kind of excellence within its own particular set of responsibilities. And from the very beginning the framers of the Master Plan acknowledged the vital role of the independent colleges and universities, envisioning higher education in California as a single continuum of educational opportunity, from small private colleges to large public universities.

- The Master Plan created, for the first time anywhere, a system that combined exceptional quality with broad access for students. This characteristic has made California the envy and exemplar of higher education not only in other states but in nations around the world. A team of international visitors from the Organization for Economic Cooperation and Development noted that California had succeeded in encouraging "constructive competition and cooperation" among its colleges and universities and praised the "complex of creativity" that characterizes California's system of higher education and makes it a model for other nations.

The remarks of the UC President represent the generally high regard in which the Master Plan and California public higher education institutions are held. As noted above, the plan and the three-tiered system it created have been evaluated and criticized over the years for different reasons. In spite of this, the combination of the UC,

---

[9]See http://www.ucop.edu/acadinit/mastplan/mpperspective.htm.

CSU, and community college system codified by the California Master Plan is considered by many to be the premier publicly funded higher education system in the world.

DoD PROFESSIONAL MILITARY EDUCATION, TRAINING, AND DEVELOPMENT SYSTEMS: THE ARMY

This section deals with the professional military education, training, and development systems in the U.S. Army. The context and the principles guiding professional military education, training, and development are the same throughout the armed forces, and the implementation of the basic principles is similar in all of the services. We use the example of the U.S. Army to illustrate the specific details of how the services treat education and training.

Background

The armed services in general, and the Army specifically, provide the military forces to deter aggression and, if necessary, to fight and win wars. The services operate in a joint (multiservice) context, and the specific vision of each service stems from *JV 2020*, a basic document for the future development of the U.S. armed forces formulated by the Joint Staff (Joint Chiefs of Staff, 2000). Thus, the "Army Vision" amounts to the Army's formulation of how the service plans to achieve the vision and the missions stipulated in *JV 2020*.

The principles of "up or out" and "educational connection to promotion" are two features of the promotion and advancement system in the armed services in general and the Army specifically. Regarding the former, personnel must advance on a clearly defined system of ranks in a certain period of time or leave the service. Regarding the latter, advancement to a higher rank carries with it a set of new responsibilities and necessitates the acquisition of additional skills and knowledge—through education and training—to enable individuals to carry out their new functions. Given such a basis for education and training, as well as the professional nature of the armed forces, all uniformed Army personnel make up the primary set of "customers" of the Army's educational institutions. Civilian employees of the Army and select personnel from the other services also attend some of the Army's educational institutions and round out the "customer" base.

Armed forces personnel remain involved continuously with the training structure of their service throughout their careers. In the Army, this spans all ranks, from the enlisted training program to noncommissioned officer (NCO) training to warrant officer training to all levels of officer training and up to and including general officer courses. Education and training in schools form one aspect of the preparation and advancement process. Field and unit training accompany most of the training in schools and provide the practical component to the formal training.

Nature of the Enterprise

The latest Army vision (formulated in 1999) contains the statement of purpose and mission for the entire organization:

> The Army is a strategic instrument of national policy, . . . safeguarding [U.S.] national interests, preventing global calamity, and making the world a safer place. [Army soldiers fulfill this mission] by finding peaceful solutions to the frictions between nation states, addressing the problems of human suffering, and when required, fighting and winning our Nation's wars. . . . The Army—while aspiring to be the most esteemed institution in the Nation . . . will remain the most respected Army in the world and the most feared ground force to those who would threaten the interests of the United States.[10]

The vision enumerates and defines seven essential characteristics of the force (responsive, deployable, agile, versatile, lethal, survivable, sustainable) required to fulfill the missions mentioned above in a joint context. The seven characteristics also serve as building blocks for the Army's development. Directions for training and education in the Army flow from the Army vision and the characteristics that the vision outlines.

The vision also contains a statement of purpose regarding the Army's educational and training system:

---

[10]Department of the Army (2000).

We are about leadership; it is our stock in trade, and it is what makes us different. We take soldiers who enter the force and grow them into leaders for the next generation of soldiers. We will continue to develop those leaders through study in the institutional schoolhouse, through field experiences gained in operational assignments, and through personal study and professional readings. Our soldiers provide back to America a corps of leaders who have an unmatched work ethic, who have a strong sense of values, who treat others with dignity and respect, who are accustomed to hard work, who are courageous, who thrive on responsibility, who know how to build and motivate teams, and who are positive role models for all around them.

Although the educational mechanisms and the training guidelines within the Army have not changed much in the past decade, the structure allows for the integration of new elements of emphasis into the education and training system. Thus, the same or similar training structures that existed in the early 1990s may change their content to adapt to the new missions and tasks—but not their form. The major focus of the Army's education and training has centered for decades on building leadership skills. As the above excerpt shows, the latest Army vision reiterates the point.

Development of the Strategic Plan

The change in Army leadership (with General Eric Shinseki taking over as the Army Chief of Staff) in 1999 provided the specific context for the formulation of the latest Army vision. In a larger sense, the combination of new technologies, a premium placed on the Army's rapid response forces during the past decade, and the absence of any "peer competitor" on the horizon, have motivated the Army to move toward a lighter and more responsive force structure and the doctrine and training to support such a force.

Shortly after his promotion, General Shinseki put together a team that worked out a new vision designed to meet the expected future challenges. The process involved input from a multitude of Army commands as well as outside experts. The vision itself amounts to a 15-paragraph statement. The general outline of the future development of the Army contained in the vision represents a major departure from the previous focus on heavy forces toward greater emphasis on "medium-weight" forces. In a nutshell, the vision represents an attempt to shift the Army's focus from heavy force-on-force engagements to a greater range of missions (from peacekeeping to high-intensity combat) with a premium placed on smaller but easier to deploy and sustain forces. General Shinseki held a news conference to announce the new vision. The concise nature of the vision and the Army's widespread coverage of it lead us to believe that all Army personnel have familiarized themselves with the vision.

General Shinseki's process for developing this vision is representative of how the Army formulates visions. Generally, a team, headed by a colonel (in this case there was also a civilian defense analyst as co-leader), is formed and a draft vision is prepared from the Chief of Staff's ideas on where the Army should be going. That draft vision is then reviewed by a large segment of the Army senior leadership and a consensus document is produced. This vision generally is "inclusive" in the sense that if a strong opinion is voiced about the inclusion of a particular idea, it is included. The advantage of such a process is that every segment of the Army can generally "find" itself in the vision. The disadvantage is that the vision that results from such a process gives little guidance to those who must make choices about funding.

Implementation and Governance

The Army vision establishes the overall evolution of the Army, but individual Army commands then work together to implement the vision and translate it into ways suitable for training the force. Decisions on the content of Army training and education and on who receives what training are inseparable from the Army's authorized manpower levels, the Army's evolving doctrine, the equipment used by the Army, and the level of resources appropriated to the Army. The Army's system of training and education involves dozens of Army commands, numerous feedback loops and, in general, is highly complex and structured. It is fully integrated into the Army's overall Planning, Programming, Budgeting, and Execution System.

Three Army offices provide most of the supervision and guidance of training and education. The Director of Training at Headquarters, Department of the Army, Office of the Deputy Chief of Staff for Operations (DCSOPS), is primarily responsible for the conduct of all Army training. The Office of the Assistant Secretary of the Army, Manpower and Reserve Affairs (ASA/MRA), contains a training division that aims to ensure the Army's effectiveness in training and education. The Office of the Deputy Chief of Staff for Personnel (DCSPER) administers pre-commissioning programs for officers (including the U.S. Military Academy) and civilian personnel training, and it manages the Army's integrated training management system, the Program for Individual Training (ARPRINT).

The Army operates dozens of schools that provide education and training. The major institutions include schools focusing on specific combat and support branches as well as institutions associated with training for specific ranks (these institutions are listed at the end of this section). In addition to these schools, the U.S. Army conducts a multitude of specialized courses at a variety of institutions and bases. The specific schools do not have visions of their own, although they do have mission statements that try to capture their essential function within the Army. For example, the U.S. Military Academy's mission is, "To educate, train, and inspire the Corps of Cadets so that each graduate is a commissioned leader of character committed to the values of Duty, Honor, Country; professional growth throughout a career as an officer in the United States Army; and a lifetime of selfless service to the nation."[11]

The number of slots for each Army training course or program and the course requirements are tied intimately to the Army's projections of skills needed and expected force levels. In short, the development of individual training requirements starts with the force structure authorization, which determines the projected unit requirements and leads to projections of the number of personnel required to staff the force (for the next seven fiscal years). In turn, that leads DCSOPS to authorize a specific number of training spaces. In a parallel process, and through a variety of tools and databases, the Total Army Personnel Command identifies the expected training and skill requirements and translates them into course requirements. Following the development of the training requirements for courses, the Army then develops a training program for each identified Military Occupational Specialty (MOS). Through a process of Structure

_____

[11]See http://www.usma.edu/mission.htm.

Manning Decision Review (SMDR), co-chaired by the DCSOPS and DCSPER, the Army then decides on establishing or altering a specific course at an Army institution to meet the requirements of the MOS.

With regard to resources, the Army manages its budget through six Program Evaluation Groups (PEGs). The training PEG manages the Army's training activities through the mechanism of some 260 Management Decision Packages (MDEPs), each of which amounts to tens or hundreds of millions of dollars. The director of training, DCSOPS, and the ASA/MRA chair the training PEG. Individual MDEP managers provide direct oversight of the Army's expenditures on training and education. Army training institutions are either MDEPs or elements of various MDEPs. Changes in resource levels occur by way of SMDR and then ARPRINT.

Several Army regulations (ARs) provide guidance for the Army's training policy and serve as the bases for development of training field manuals to put the policies into practice: AR-350-1 (*Army Training*), AR-350-10 (*Management of Army Individual Training Requirements*), AR-350-38 (*Training Device Policies and Management*), AR-350-41 (*Training in Units*), and AR-351-1 (*Individual Military Education and Training*). All training regulations include objectives, policies, guidance, and a delineation of responsibilities for the conduct and management of training. The Army's TRADOC manages the training development system. Through the service schools, TRADOC develops training materials for Army-wide use. In the realm of training, these include two main field manuals (FMs): FM 25-100 (*Training the Force)* and FM 25-101 (*Battle-Focused Training)*.

Evaluation of Organizational Performance

With the vision in place, the Army component commands have begun to translate the vision into specific tasks in their own areas of responsibility. Because the educational and training elements of the Army do not form one whole but are themselves parts of larger components of a highly integrated organization, it is impossible to speak of any specific plan in the training realm designed to implement the vision. Instead, each of the hundreds of educational and training elements of the Army, over time, will adopt changes in course content that reflect the overall direction presented in the vision. As outlined above, implementing the vision entails a process of developing requirements and then staffing and funding them, led by DCSOPS and DCSPER. The process is essentially mandate-based. As Army forces move toward exhibiting more of the seven characteristics outlined in the vision, their progress in that direction is monitored and harmonized with other elements of the Army. As the Army moves toward adapting the elements of the vision into its everyday operations, evaluations of performance also will take into account proficiency at tasks tied to the characteristics that the vision outlines.

Schools Operated by the U.S. Army

- Army War College (including the Department of Corresponding Studies and the Strategic Studies Institute),

- Army Command and General Staff College (including the Combined Arms Services Staff School and the School of Advanced Military Studies),

- U.S. Military Academy,

- Army Logistics Management College,

- Army Management Staff College (AMSC),

- Fort Gordon, Georgia, U.S. Army Signal Center,

- Soldier Support Institute (including the U.S. Army Adjutant General School, the U.S. Army Finance School, the NCO Academy at Fort Jackson, South Carolina, and the U.S. Army Recruiting and Retention School at Fort Jackson),

- Fort Sill, Oklahoma, NCO Academy,

- Judge Advocate General's School,

- National Simulation Center,

- Ordnance Missile and Munitions Center and School,

- Peacekeeping Institute,

- Ranger Training Brigade,

- Redstone Scientific Information Center,

- Maneuver Support Center and Fort Leonard Wood, Missouri (including the U.S. Army Chemical School, the U.S. Army Engineer School, and the U.S. Army Military Police School),

- U.S. Army Air Defense Artillery School, Fort Bliss, Texas,

- U.S. Army Aeromedical Center, Fort Rucker, Alabama,

- U.S. Army Armor Center, Fort Knox, Kentucky,

- U.S. Army Aviation Center and School and Fort Rucker,

- U.S. Army Aviation Logistics School,

- U.S. Army Field Artillery Training Center and School,

- U.S. Army Physical Fitness School,

- U.S. Army Infantry Center and School,

- U.S. Army Intelligence School,

- U.S. Army Materiel Command School of Engineering and Logistics,

- U.S. Army Medical Department Center and School,

- U.S. Army Medical Research Institute of Chemical Defense,

- U.S. Army Military History Institute, and

- U.S. Army Sergeants Major Academy.

AMERICAN MEDICAL ASSOCIATION

Background

Since 1847, the AMA has strived to be the principal voice of the medical profession and medical education in the United States. In 1942, the AMA Council on Medical Education and the Association of American Medical Colleges established the Liaison Committee on Medical Education, which maintains standards for undergraduate programs and accredits the 125 U.S. and 16 Canadian medical schools offering medical degrees.[12] The AMA's commitment to ed-

---

[12] See http://www.americanmedicalassociation.org.

ucation extends to the graduate medical and continuing medical education. The Accreditation Council for Graduate Medical Education, sponsored by the AMA and four other organizations, accredits nearly 7,700 residency programs in 1,600 medical institutions across the country. In addition, through the Accreditation Council on Continuing Medical Education, the AMA participates in accrediting institutions that offer continuing medical education programs for physicians. Through working with these affiliated organizations, the AMA exerts an extensive effect on medical education and is arguably the most influential medical organization in the United States.

In 1997, the AMA began to realize that there were gaps and redundancies in responsibilities within the AMA that led to some areas being ignored and others being pursued by people with different reporting chains. Therefore, in 1998, the AMA's Ad Hoc Committee on Structure, Governance, and Operations, with the help of an outside consulting company, conducted a study on internal governance within the AMA,[13] identifying areas of weakness. This study found:

- Overlapping and insufficient definitions of roles and responsibilities among the different governing entities within the AMA,

- Self-interest occasionally taking precedence over organizational priorities, and

- Inadequate involvement of all internal and external stakeholders.

The committee also examined the AMA's strategic planning process, which is the responsibility of the 20-member board of trustees. The committee found that the strategies listed in the planning process lacked sufficient detail, including a relevant time frame for accomplishing them; there was not enough information on how the strategy implementation would be evaluated; the plan was not well integrated with the AMA's day-to-day work; and the plan was overly focused on short-term needs. The AMA therefore undertook an effort to improve its strategic planning process.

---

[13]Nelson (1998).

Nature of the Enterprise

In response to the 1998 study, the AMA updated its values, vision, and objectives. The three core values of the AMA are "1) leadership and service; 2) excellence in all we do; and 3) integrity and ethical behavior." AMA's long-term vision is "to be an essential part of the professional life of every physician and an essential force for progress in improving the nation's health." Four key objectives flow from this vision:

The AMA will pursue being

1. The world's leader in obtaining, synthesizing, integrating, and disseminating information on health and medical practice;
2. The acknowledged leader in setting standards for medical ethics, practice, and education;
3. The most authoritative voice and influential advocate for patients and physicians; and
4. A sound organization that provides value to members, federation organizations, and employees.

Development of the Strategic Plan

The board of trustees is the chief planning agent for the AMA, developing both the annual plan and the budget. The AMA's board has constructed four strategic planning elements:

1. Establish a core purpose and value,
2. Identify a vision for the future,
3. Identify objectives to achieve the vision, and
4. Develop key strategies to achieve the objectives.

These four elements are reflected in the AMA strategic plan. First, it uses information as the foundation for the development of strategic directions and plans. Second, it garners broad participation by both internal and external stakeholders who provide input on setting strategic directions and priorities. Third, it has created a process to set the both short- and long-term strategic directions of the association. The process includes gaining input from all stakeholders. The strategic directions are both long-term and short-term.

The AMA's strategic planning efforts are on an annual cycle. In its advisory role, the Council on Long-Range Planning and Development conducts studies on emerging issues and environmental trends and is the strategic support mechanism for the board. Early in the year, the board of trustees reviews reports prepared by the council, core purposes, objectives, and past performance and then revises strategic directions. Other internal stakeholders provide their input at this time. During the spring and summer, projects for resource planning for the following year are discussed and approved.

Implementation and Governance

The executive vice president, leading approximately 1,200 staff members, is in charge of running the daily operations of the AMA. The AMA has made improvements to its extensive governance system that includes the 20-member board of trustees, a 400-member house of delegates, and several councils. Members of the house of delegates[14] serve as an important communications, policy, and membership link between the AMA and grassroots physicians. Delegates are AMA members who are either elected or selected by a sponsoring organization (such as a hospital). The house of delegates nominates members for various councils, such as the Council on Medical Education. These councils monitor policies under their purview.

According to board policy, all the activities pursued by the AMA staff, board members, delegates, and council members should be linked to their strategic plan. There are two ways in which these links are es-

---

[14]These members regularly communicate AMA policy, information, activities, and programs to constituents; relate constituent views to the appropriate AMA leadership, governing body, or executive staff; advocate constituent views within the house of delegates; attend and report highlights of house of delegates meetings to constituents, for example, at hospital medical staff, county, state and specialty society meetings; serve as advocates for patients to improve the health of the public and the health care system; cultivate promising leaders for all levels of organized medicine and help them gain leadership positions; actively recruit new AMA members and help retain current members; and participate in the AMA Membership Outreach Program.

tablished. First, each of the four key objectives in the AMA vision is pursued through a set of strategies that serve to further define the specific pursuit of each objective. Thirteen strategies (arrayed under the four objectives) provide the basis for developing specific programs and budgets. For example, under the objective to be the world's leader in obtaining, synthesizing, integrating, and disseminating information on health and medical practices, one strategy is to provide physicians with timely, accurate, and relevant information on health science and medical practice. Under the objective of being the acknowledged leader in setting standards for medical ethics, practice, and education, one strategy is to set, disseminate, and apply standards of medical practice to help physicians provide the best possible care to patients.

Second, the board of trustees ensures that all AMA projects are consistent with AMA's overall goals. To accomplish this objective, the board defines the mission and actions of different internal committees for consistency with the strategic plan. Furthermore, all resolutions submitted to the AMA house of delegates are generally required to identify the specific component of the AMA strategic plan that the resolution addresses.

Evaluation of Organizational Performance

The AMA has created a process to evaluate the success of implementing and achieving the association's strategic plan. The board of trustees has oversight of this task but must periodically disseminate status reports to the house of delegates. In addition to the board's own assessment, the AMA conducts an externally based evaluation of the extent to which the board and its members exerted a positive influence on the key objectives and strategies defined in the AMA's strategic plan.

Discussion

It is telling that even this large, powerful organization has had difficulties with strategic planning. Specifically, an evaluation committee found that a prior strategic plan lacked sufficient detail and was somewhat divorced from day-to-day activities. Including specific details can be a very important, but sometimes neglected, strategic planning component. For example, strategic plans should include time frames to help orient staff to deadlines. Without time frames, there may be no sense of urgency in meeting objectives. Similarly, a strategic plan should include a process for evaluating whether the objectives have been achieved. If the evaluation component is missing, there may be a concurrent sense that achieving the objectives is not important. On another note, connecting the plan to day-to-day work activities can be quite challenging. If done on a superficial level, it can be relatively easy to compose a vision, mission, objectives, strategy, and even an evaluation component, but it is quite another accomplishment to ensure that day-to-day work activities are connected to the values, vision, and mission. The AMA is attempting to make these connections through the work of its board, its house of delegates, and its staff. These three bodies must think regularly of their work in terms of the strategic plan. The hope is that this extra effort will ensure that all activities address issues of core importance to the AMA.

QUALITY ASSURANCE AGENCY

Background

The Quality Assurance Agency for Higher Education was established in 1997 to provide an integrated quality assurance service for higher education institutions in the United Kingdom. The QAA is an independent body with seven staff members funded mainly by subscriptions from universities and colleges to review the performance of the higher education institutions in the British system. It performs these reviews by assessing the quality and standards of teaching and learning at both the subject and the institution level. The results of these audits and assessments are distributed to the public and maintained on the agency's web page.

Nature of the Enterprise

The agency's mission is "to promote public confidence that quality of provision and standards of awards in higher education are being safeguarded and enhanced." It fulfills this mission by:

- "working with higher education institutions to promote and support continuous improvement in the quality and standards of provision;

- providing clear and accurate information to students, employers, and others about the quality and standards of higher education provision;

- working with higher education institutions to develop and manage the qualifications framework;

- advising on the grant of degree awarding powers and university title;

- facilitating the development of benchmark information to guide subject standards;

- promulgating codes of practice and examples of good practice; and

- operating programs of review of performance at institutional and program levels."[15]

Development of the Strategic Plan

The board of directors, consisting of 14 members, has the responsibility of developing and managing the strategic direction of the agency. A recent internal audit conducted by agency staff suggested the need for a three-year strategic plan. Subsequently, the board analyzed environmental trends and sought assistance from key stakeholders, such as college presidents, student representatives, professional societies, and employers. Agency objectives and budget were developed from the mission statement, environmental trends, and stakeholder input.

Examples of agency objectives include the number of subject reviews it will undertake; the number of institutional audits it will conduct; the completion of a handbook to guide institutions through the review processes; a time frame for the selection, appointing, and

---

[15]See http://www.qaa.ac.uk/aboutqaa/aboutQAA.htm.

training of reviewers; and a process for soliciting feedback from stakeholders.

The next steps for the agency in developing its planning capacity include developing the supporting resource strategies to allow the agency to deliver its plan; embedding progress monitoring and reporting systems; strengthening the links between organizational, directorate, team, and individual objectives; and strengthening the links between planning and budgeting.

Implementation and Governance

The board has two specific responsibilities that ensure the enactment of their strategic plan. First, they regularly review the agency's policies, vision, values, and overall strategic direction. Second, they monitor performance against agreed-upon strategic objectives and targets.

Evaluation of Organizational Performance

An internal audit committee advises the board on the effectiveness of the agency's internal control systems and the arrangements to promote economy, efficiency, and effectiveness in the agency. In addition, the agency conducts self-evaluation through an external audit. The results are published in an annual report, which includes a full description of the agency's role, activities, and plans, and comments on the extent to which key strategic objectives and agreed-upon financial and other performance targets have been met.

The agency achieved its strategic objectives for 1998–1999. These objectives included conducting subject reviews and disseminating the findings; planning for 375 subject reviews to be conducted in 1999–2000; reviewing degree-awarding powers; performing and evaluating trials of a new academic review method; and finalizing plans for staff performance review and professional development.

Discussion

The Quality Assurance Agency does not make any major decisions without substantial input from its stakeholders. Such continuous feedback, coupled with the funding it receives from the higher education community, has led to a level of legitimacy that allows the agency to conduct its reviews without encountering organizational resistance.

Its strategic planning process has forced the agency to decide which institutions will be reviewed at what level and what resources will be needed for these reviews. The board is instrumental in monitoring the implementation of the strategic plan. This plan is published on its web page and distributed to all stakeholders so that everyone is aware of current and future activities. The use of its web page has increased its ability to provide feedback to stakeholders.

CASE STUDIES FROM SITE VISITS

KENTUCKY COUNCIL FOR POSTSECONDARY EDUCATION

Background

The Kentucky higher education system currently consists of eight universities—two research (University of Louisville and University of Kentucky (UK), both of which have extensive academic health centers) and six regional comprehensive universities—and a system of 28 community and technical colleges. This reflects the combination of two systems that had been separate before 1997. Community colleges had been under the jurisdiction of the University of Kentucky, whereas the technical colleges were the responsibility of the Workforce Development Cabinet. Some community and technical colleges will eventually merge and consolidate locally, with one president, so their number will drop.

In 1996, the Kentucky General Assembly adopted Senate Concurrent Resolution 93, which created the Task Force on Postsecondary Education. The task force commissioned an assessment of postsecondary education in Kentucky, and the assessment report was published in March 1997. The report painted a dismal picture of Kentucky's educational attainment. It emphasized the existence of many unproductive (defined as graduating few students per year), low-performing, and duplicative programs, and a lack of strategic vision for postsecondary education. Of particular concern were program duplication and a lack of transferability between the community college and technical college systems. Another concern related to the formula funding system that rewarded growth, encouraged add-ons, and encouraged institutions to compete for the same students. Furthermore, student retention was not a critical issue in the formula system in place in 1997.

In addition, the report strongly criticized the Council of Higher Education (CHE) (created in 1934) for a lack of leadership on higher education issues. In the report, the task force asserted that credible leadership was needed to develop and implement a statewide educational mission and to promote strategic financial planning.

The task force report suggested that the education system be linked to state priorities, that the system should be coordinated and performance reviewed, and that the finance structure should direct funds toward the state's strategic goals. In response, the state passed the Postsecondary Improvement Act, also known as House Bill 1 (HB1) in May 1997. It established six goals for the state to achieve by 2020:

1. A seamless, integrated system of postsecondary education planned and funded to enhance economic development and the quality of life.

2. The University of Kentucky will be ranked among the top 20 public comprehensive research universities in the country.

3. The University of Louisville will be nationally recognized as a premier metropolitan research university.

4. Regional universities will have at least one nationally recognized program of distinction or applied research program and will work cooperatively with other institutions to ensure access to quality baccalaureate and master's level education.

5. A comprehensive community and technical college system that promotes access to general education, workforce training, remedial education, and continuing education.

6. An efficient, responsive, and coordinated system of autonomous institutions delivering educational services to citizens in a quantity and quality comparable to national averages.

The bill transformed the CHE organization although the new organization kept many of the same people. HB1 changed the name to the

Council for Postsecondary Education (CPE) and it charged CPE with developing and implementing a strategic agenda and performance indicators to track the progress of the six goals. HB1 also created and gave CPE control over the allocation of incentive funds.

In the process of revamping the council, there was a clear attempt to reestablish its credibility through respected new leadership. HB1 changed the title of the head of CPE to president and mandated that the salary of the position would be greater than that of any of the presidents of the educational institutions. These statutory provisions were designed to elevate the power of the CPE president over that of institution heads. In selecting a president of CPE, the search committee wanted someone with a national reputation to improve the prestige of the system, and Gordon Davies was identified as a good match.

Nature of the Enterprise

The current governor, Governor Patton, is very supportive of education and wants to be known as the education governor. His motto is "Education Pays," and this motto is visible all over the state. The governor's vision is to emphasize the link between education and economic development. He also stresses that access without quality is mediocrity and quality without access is elitism.

House Bill 1 laid the groundwork for higher education planning in the state. It spelled out the vision for the state but gave CPE responsibility for developing follow-on documents, such as a strategic agenda, a strategic implementation plan, and performance indicators. In response to that mandate, CPE spent six months gathering input from a wide range of its stakeholders and ultimately published *2020 Vision: An Agenda for Kentucky's System of Higher Education* (Kentucky Council on Postsecondary Education, 1998). This document articulated to the public what it could expect of the state's higher education system.

2020 Vision asks the state's citizens to envision the following:

- Educated citizens who want advanced knowledge and skills and know how to acquire them; and who are good parents, good citizens, and economically self-sufficient workers.

- Globally competitive businesses and industries respected for their highly knowledgeable employees and the technological sophistication of their products and services.

- Vibrant communities offering a standard of living unsurpassed by those in other states and nations.

- Scholars and practitioners who are among the best in the world, dedicated to creating new ideas, technologies, and knowledge.

- An integrated system of elementary and secondary schools and providers of postsecondary education, committed to meeting the needs of students and the Commonwealth, and acclaimed for excellence, innovation, collaboration, and responsiveness.

The vision grew out of comparisons between where Kentucky was (in terms of per capita income and educational attainment) and national averages. The state's goal is to bring the standard of living for the state of Kentucky up to the national average. It is trying to address two issues: Jobs must exist or educated people will leave, and educated people must be found to fill those jobs. The education goals fit in neatly with the state's larger vision. However, CPE considers the vision to be dynamic, as it must reflect what is happening in the state and legislative priorities (which CPE, in turn, tries to influence).

The University of Kentucky Survey Research Center polled Kentucky citizens (including legislators, community leaders, and others, to get a range of views) about what they consider to be important goals for the state. The results showed that education, the environment, participatory government, and other quality-of-life issues led the list. In addition, CPE has identified some of what it views as Kentucky's key issues. CPE believes that there is an education deficit in the population and that there is a fixed population (the state is not growing). So the council wants to reward not only enrollment growth but also program completion. Also, CPE wants the University of Kentucky to have more graduate and professional students. Although there has been a tendency for the universities to complain about the level of funding provided to the institutions, Gordon Davies argues that the system is adequately funded.[1] He thinks they can do a lot more with the money they are currently spending.

The vast majority (83 percent) of Kentuckians say that they are satisfied with their quality of life, yet 25 percent lack even a high school diploma. Focus groups and surveys indicate that people are primarily motivated to attend college by the promise of better pay. The state must deal with "placedness"—that is, parents not wanting their children to go away to school. The family culture is such that education is not encouraged.

Development of the Strategic Plan

CPE wrote an action agenda that addresses how it will implement the 2020 Vision document over the next four years. In it, CPE set enrollment, retention, and graduation goals. The action agenda spells out what CPE needs to do, what institutions need to do, and what the government needs to do. In addition, each institution has written a brief description of its plans to conform to the action agenda. Each of the institutions' two-page action agendas addresses the following topics: Why is it important for Kentucky to have this institution as one of its universities? How will this university enroll, retain, and graduate more students? How will this university and the publics it serves become more engaged with one another? How will this university know whether it has done what it says it will do? Variations on these topics are addressed by the comprehensive universities, research universities, the Kentucky Community and Technical College System, the Kentucky Commonwealth Virtual University, and the state's independent colleges and universities.

Implementation and Governance

The transformation of CHE into CPE did not involve a major governance change, but it did make the system more market-driven. Since the governor has made education reform his legacy, the position of CPE president is close to the top of the state hierarchy (see Figure C.1), reporting directly to a member of the governor's office. The

---

[1]Gordon Davies granted permission to attribute statements to him.

RAND *MR1234-C.1*

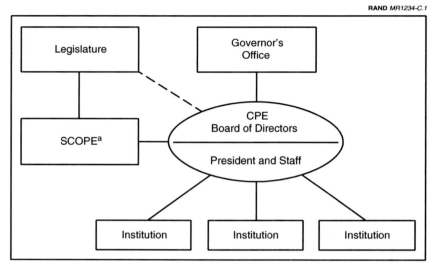

^a Strategic Committee on Post-secondary Education.

Figure C.1—The Kentucky Council for Postsecondary Education

council is considered a cabinet-level office and is part of the executive branch of state government. Much of the real "power" of CPE comes from the support of the governor.

CPE is a coordinating board, not a governing board, and as such wields both official and unofficial power. Some of the official purposes of CPE include—provide factual information to state political leaders, adopt a statewide agenda that provides direction to the system, and eliminate duplication and wasteful competition. The CPE staff makes biennial budget recommendations to the state legislature and recommendations regarding space, capital, and operating budgets. CPE has the authority to approve new programs and close down existing ones (although it rarely does so). It can also set minimum admission requirements. It licenses out-of-state institutions that operate within Kentucky.

CPE's control over funding was also changed by HB1. In the past, schools were funded on a per-student basis, irrespective of where students were from or what they were studying. Now funding is based on enrollment characteristics (e.g., targeted enrollment, such as students from underserved areas) and student retention. Some money is still put into base funds based on enrollment, and CPE uses the remaining money as incentive funds to bring about change.

Because of CPE's limited official power over institutions, Davies has developed unofficial techniques for influencing the institutions. He believes that he can be most effective by working to keep the institutions on their toes—stirring things up occasionally and getting the institutions to react. He also considers information an important source of power. He wants the CPE to know more than the institutions know and to use the information effectively.

Davies also believes in consensus building, and inspiring the institution leaders as a group. He has monthly meetings with the institution presidents, and other CPE staff meet regularly with the academic affairs officers from the institutions (there is no equivalent group for the finance officers). In cases where CPE deems it necessary to impose penalties, it withholds money from the incentive funds or publicizes program or institutional performance, even when it is poor.

The above figure also depicts SCOPE, which was initially formed to conduct the search for a president for CPE. The group is composed of the governor, general assembly leadership, and staff of CPE. SCOPE's purpose now is to ensure that elected leaders play a role in developing the strategic agenda for postsecondary education. To some extent, the need for SCOPE reflected the failure of CHE. Since the creation of CPE has addressed that problem, there is some question about SCOPE's future role.

Quality and Productivity Evaluation

CPE is responsible for developing performance measures. There has been discussion within CPE about how to measure quality, since it is difficult to define the concept of quality in absolute terms. Davies is interested in measuring value-added and "fitness for purpose," since there is no single definition of quality that will work for all institutions.

CPE is able to measure the progress of the state's institutions against national averages and against similar information from other states.

Kentucky has expanded the list of states with which it compares itself. Davies said it is no longer good enough to compare Kentucky to Mississippi, Alabama, and Arkansas. Now, state officials are also looking at North Carolina, Ohio, and Virginia. They have a benchmark list of comparison institutions for each university—this is their first effort at national benchmarking and it relates to their interest in developing premier institutions.

Davies has outlined four standards that reflect the action agenda goals: Take more students in, keep them in, make employers happy, and make students into lifelong learners. The metrics are easy for such statistics as completion rates and enrollment rates but more difficult for measuring the achievement of broader social goals. For quality-of-life measures, they look at such resources as *The Kids Count Data Book*, published by the Annie E. Casey Foundation (Kentucky ranks in the 40s on this book's scales). Specific targets have been established for total public and private undergraduate enrollment growth, 1998 through 2020; undergraduate enrollment for each institution, 1998 through 2004; graduate and professional enrollment for the University of Kentucky and University of Louisville, 1998 through 2006; retention rates for each institution, 1998 through 2006; baccalaureate graduation rates, 1998 through 2006; and statewide college-going rates (compared to the national average), 1998 through 2006.

CPE will also assess progress toward the system's strategic goals by looking at how individual institutions, and groups of institutions (such as the community and technical colleges and private institutions), progress toward their respective goals. As noted, in each institution's or group's action agenda, evidence for determining "How will we know whether we have done what we say we will do?" is described. The following are examples from several different action agendas:

How will UK know that it has done what it says it will do?

- Systematic assessment of results; comparison of results to goals in the strategic plan, and

- Annual strategic plan progress report presented to the board of trustees.

How will the University of Louisville know whether it has done what it says it will do?

- By measuring the university's accomplishment of the goals it has identified,

- By gauging, from various economic, cultural, and civic indicators, the health of the metropolitan region and the university's effect on it, and

- By attaining membership of the Brandeis School of Law in the Order of the Coif (the premier honorary professional society for law).

From the Kentucky Community and Technical College System—how will you know whether you have done what you say you will do?

- Increase student referrals and assessments,

- Expand secondary and baccalaureate transfer agreements—and ensure transfer within the system, and

- Increase enrollment by 5,000 students by 2002.

These agendas offer varying degrees of specificity but can still guide CPE as it tries to measure progress toward the system's strategic goals.

Discussion

Because of the limits on the CPE president's control, he has developed indirect ways of exerting authority over the institutions in his purview. He considers the basis of his influence to be the value he can offer institutions, whether through advocacy to the legislature and the public, increased funding, or other types of support. When he first assumed his position, he visited every campus, and since then he has met monthly with institution heads. This helps him to know his institutions well, including their strengths and vulnerabilities. On an individual, personal basis, he uses several leadership techniques, such as offering quality ideas and good data. The CPE president also works to create synergies in relationships and to link reforms with other efforts.

In terms of promoting the system as a whole, CPE has worked to build a strong constituency for its reform efforts, so that its work will outlast the tenure of its current staff. CPE has set objectives with specific measures and benchmarks and compares its practices with best practices. Stakeholder involvement has also been a priority for CPE, so its leadership encourages using focus groups with stake-holders and using advisory committees to solicit input.

TEXAS HIGHER EDUCATION COORDINATING BOARD

Background

The Texas higher education system consists of 120 institutions—three-fourths are public or private four-year institutions and one-fourth consists of technical or community colleges—serving 966,840 students. More than half (54 percent) of these students are enrolled in either public or private four-year institutions; 46 percent are en-rolled in community or technical colleges. The state expects enroll-ment to continue increasing in public institutions by 5 percent over the next five years.

The Texas Higher Education Coordinating Board (CB) is a state agency that was created by the Texas legislature in 1965 to ensure quality and efficiency in public higher education. With the senate's recommendations, the governor appoints 18 trustees, representing all areas of the state, to oversee the board. Trustees appoint a com-missioner of higher education as the chief administrator for the agency. The board has 278 full-time budgeted positions.

The CB, like all other state agencies, submits its annual budget to the house, which has the authority to approve, disapprove, or change the budget request. The house then passes the revised budget to the senate for approval. Figure C.2 illustrates these relationships, includ-ing an illustration of how the board relates to sister organizations, such as the Texas Workforce Commission and the board of educa-tion.

The current commissioner of higher education was appointed in 1997. The new commissioner believed that the board was not effec-tive in identifying its focus and viewed strategic planning as a means for rectifying that situation. In addition, the new commissioner

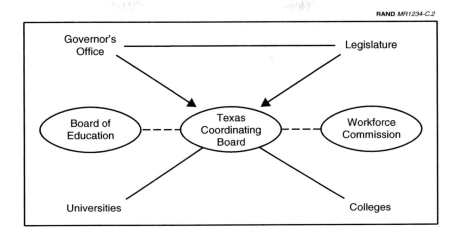

Figure C.2—The Texas Higher Education Coordinating Board

wanted to aggressively narrow the gap between Texas and peer states, in terms of matriculation, retention, and graduation rates. He again considered the development of a strategic plan as a first step in closing that gap. Past CB planning efforts have been episodic, overly ambitious, vague, and misguided. These past efforts, however, have provided useful lessons in strategic planning.

Nature of the Enterprise

The board's core values include quality education and service to the student and community. The board's mission is "to provide the Legislature advice and comprehensive capability for higher education, to coordinate the effective delivery of higher education, to administer efficiently assigned statewide programs, and to advance higher education for the people of Texas."

The board has several roles, including reviewing and recommending changes in formulas for allocation of state funds to public institutions; authorizing and reviewing academic and technical programs to ensure quality; working to eliminate costly duplication in academic and technical programs; developing plans to ensure quality in Texas public higher education; developing a performance information system for the universities and community and technical colleges, including comparative financial, performance, and cost information; and administering the state's student financial aid program.

Development of the Strategic Plan

Development of the board's 2001–2005 strategic plan began in 1997, when CB staff reviewed their responsibilities. A memo was then sent to chancellors and presidents of Texas public higher education institutions, inviting review and written comment on the responsibilities of the board. This memo was the beginning of a sustained effort to gather substantial external input. The CB created a large planning committee dedicated to this effort consisting of 24 people:

- The vice chair of the board,

- Six current board members,

- Several former coordinating board members,

- Governing board members (from the universities and colleges),

- Business people and representatives of the community,

- Former chancellor of a university, and

- Former president of a community college.

Broad participation on this committee has led to the development of a consensus on the CB's goals through accommodating a diverse group of people. In addition to involving stakeholders through this committee, the commissioner of the coordinating board has had roundtables with institutional governing boards, presidents, and chancellors about what the most important goals should be.

CB members and the strategic planning committee have held several meetings to discuss internal and external threats and opportunities. These meetings have also resulted in much discussion on the linkages between the state's higher education needs and the board's efforts. These meetings culminated in a strategic plan for 1999–2003, which was updated and changed to a plan for 2001–2005.

The plan for 2001–2005 is based on the board's mission, philosophy, scope, functions, statutory responsibilities, and external and internal threats and opportunities delineated by the strategic planning committee. The strategic plan has six goals:

1. To coordinate higher education in Texas and promote quality and access in all aspects of higher education.

2. To make loans available to college students who need financial assistance to attend college.

3. To provide state funding to institutions and students through a variety of special programs designed to improve the quality and delivery of instruction, increase access to higher education, improve health care in Texas, and facilitate research at Texas institutions.

4. To provide programs to improve the delivery and quality of higher education and increase access to higher education.

5. To provide federal funding to institutions and students to improve higher education in Texas.

6. To include historically underutilized businesses in the total value of purchasing contracts awarded annually.

Implementation and Governance

Each of the goals identified above is accompanied by corresponding objectives specifying how the goal will be accomplished, preset criteria against which to measure performance on the objectives, and strategies for meeting the objectives. For example, under the first goal of coordinating higher education in Texas and promoting quality and access in all aspects of higher education, one objective is "to promote quality in all aspects of public higher education including teaching, research, and public service." A strategy for reaching this objective is to coordinate and evaluate university programs. The board staff will know they have achieved this strategy by the number of programs they have reviewed in a preset time frame.

Evaluation of Organizational Performance

The state of Texas has implemented a Performance Based Funding System. This is a statewide program for all state agencies receiving appropriated funds from the state. This system requires that each agency, including the board, articulate its goals and propose measures of those goals. The board has done that by developing its strategic plan. If these goals are unmet, some funding may be withheld by the state. Achievement of goals contained in the 2001–2005 plan has not yet been evaluated.

Discussion

The Texas Higher Education Coordinating Board has been in existence for 35 years and continues to update and improve its strategic planning process. Its experience underscores how challenging the process can be. Past planning efforts have been both overly optimistic and have lacked the detail necessary for implementation. In other words, past strategic plans have promised a grandiose mansion without an accompanying blueprint. The board now uses its current strategic planning process as a mechanism for prioritizing and focusing its goals and then ensuring that these goals are indeed met. It has solicited input and feedback on its goals throughout the creation of its strategic plan. The State legislature will hold the board accountable for meeting its goals.

DEPARTMENT OF TRANSPORTATION

Background

Under the leadership of Secretary Rodney Slater, the Department of Transportation has pursued an overarching management strategy designed to develop an integrated and unified department, or "One DoT," where intermodal collaboration and partnership between the OAs will provide the highest quality transportation system for the country. Building on the One DoT concept, the department has identified 60 flagship goals, based on its strategic plan, that unify the OAs in vision for One DoT success in the next two years. Included in these flagship goals are workforce planning and employee development, which are both high-priority initiatives across the department.

As Figure C.3 illustrates, DoT education and professional development policy are coordinated through the L&D program in the Office of Human Resource Management. The office provides policy guidance and recommendations to the OAs through a collaborative effort with the OA representatives who serve on a Learning and Development Council. Members of the human resources department from each OA represent their respective agencies on the council and provide input and feedback on education and development policies for the department as a whole. Implementation of education and professional development activities takes place at the OA-level, and the L&D program has no direct control or authority over what is carried out. In this way, the L&D program office can be seen as analogous to the Chancellor's office, because OA training offices do not report to the L&D program, nor does the L&D program have any control over training budgets. Despite its limited authority, the L&D program is still responsible for guiding the education and professional development activities for the department as a whole.

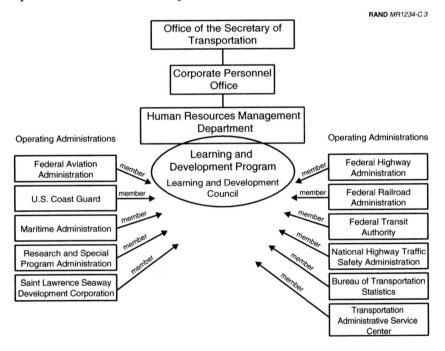

RAND *MR1234-C.3*

Figure C.3—The DoT Education and Professional Development Context

The following notes summarize an interview conducted with staff in DoT's L&D program, offering a general picture of the strategic planning for DoT as a whole as well as for education and professional development activities going on in the department. This general policy overview is followed by notes from an interview with one of DoT's OAs—the FHWA—and outlines how it has undertaken the implementation of its education and development activities more specifically.

Nature of the Enterprise

The vision of DoT is to be "a visionary and vigilant Department of Transportation leading the way to transportation excellence in the twenty-first century."

DoT's mission is to "serve the United States by ensuring a fast, safe, efficient, accessible, and convenient transportation system that meets our vital national interests and enhances the quality of life of the American people, today and into the future" (DoT, 1997).

Development of the Strategic Plan

In the past, strategic planning was undertaken separately by each OA; for example, the FHWA did its own strategic planning, as did the Federal Aviation Administration, the Coast Guard, and so on. The passage of the GPRA in 1993 forced heterogeneous agencies such as DoT to think more intermodally, or across transportation modes, because separate OAs have to be accountable for their effect on overall DoT performance and results. Under the GPRA, OAs must now articulate their missions as part of the overall mission of DoT and take into account reciprocal performance effects across OAs. Some cross-cutting areas are safety, infrastructure, and mobility, which are common to all transportation modes.

In conjunction with the strategic plan required under the GPRA, the major departmental initiative, "One DoT" unifies the OAs in vision through 60 flagship goals that the DoT secretary has laid out to accomplish over two years. Organized around the six strategic goals outlined in the DoT plan, the flagship goals include workforce planning and employee development under the DoT-wide corporate management strategy. As the strategic objective for human resource development, the employee development flagship goal is to "ensure a continuous learning environment required of all high performing organizations by implementing policies, providing resources and opportunities that enable all DoT employees to build the job competencies, technical capabilities, leadership and management skills, and organizational knowledge required to achieve strategic goals" (DoT, 1999).

Up until the mid-1990s, DoT had a centralized training unit; it then decentralized that function, so that it had virtually no intermodal sharing for professional development purposes. A key goal for the recentralized L&D unit is to find shared themes—what the various organizations under DoT can learn from each other and how to provide a One DoT flavor to key competencies.

It was critical to make a link between strategic planning and learning and development. Making the link required a shift of focus from "training" to "learning"—a big cultural difference. It also required connecting learning, in the minds of line managers, to the strategic plans required by the GPRA. Suggestions for how to strategically align learning and development activities with agency mission and goals were developed by a task force headed by a representative of the L&D program (Human Resource Development Council, 1997). That report closely connects learning goals to performance improvement set out in President Clinton's and Vice President Gore's Blair House Papers (Clinton, 1997).

The current secretary of transportation has boosted the One DoT concept to raise the visibility of learning and its connection to mission performance. With his support, the Human Resource Management Department produced a conceptual framework intended as a tool to link employee development to workforce planning as well as performance results in concrete ways. The framework directly reflects the strategic orientation of the Blair House Papers and the companion report "Getting Results Through Learning" (Human Resource Development Council, 1997).

Implementation and Governance

General decisionmaking responsibility for the department is managed by the Office of the Secretary of Transportation (OST), which oversees policy issues for the entire department. The strategic plan is being implemented by OST in response to the requirements of the GPRA. In addition to the five-year strategic plan required under the GPRA, federal agencies must also submit annual performance plans and performance reports with their budget requests to Congress. These documents will "serve as a link between strategic goals, annual goals and the DoT program activity structure—[the 10 OAs and 140 budgeted program activities]" (DoT, 1997). Ultimately, Congress deems the plans a success or failure.

There has been some difficulty in plan implementation at the level of learning and professional development because managers are not always aware of the content of the strategic plan and its connection to human resource issues. The aim of the L&D program has been to get learning and development goals to be a part of OA managers' daily work through orientation training and the L&D council members. Some resistance from the older employees toward the new management practices has also made implementation more difficult.

The L&D program has no formal authority except for appropriations law that specifies how training dollars must be used. These are very general stipulations, requiring, for instance, that employees understand the purpose of the training, that courses be evaluated at some level, and that training not cause undue stress or be in conflict with employees' values.

According to the DoT L&D program, the learning and development policies set forth in the framework are not resisted by the OAs, because the OAs are looking for ideas about how to do things well and how to get the most out of their L&D program. The individual OAs can mandate training practices and policy for the programs and offices within their administration. For example, the U.S. Coast Guard adopted the Kirkpatrick model for evaluation and requires it for all of its training activities.

Involvement in the L&D council helps OAs feel some ownership of the recommended policies and strategies. The program office is trying to develop a performance consulting approach where it has a participatory role rather than adopting a command and control mentality.

A problem identified by the L&D program is that the department does not learn as One DoT. There are areas where OAs' missions overlap ("intermodalism") and where it would be possible to establish cross-cutting learning and development activities. The system is currently decentralized, but the Human Resources Office is trying to develop One DoT development activities where appropriate.

Some OAs have their own academies or institutes. However, because of resource constraints, most learning and development activities are done externally. OAs select vendors of training and learning programs through their regular procurement processes. The L&D program staff are trying to find ways to share resources for the One DoT cross-cutting learning and development courses. They are using the University of Maryland to help create these common courses. Once they develop a One DoT learning plan, they will need to sell the L&D council on the common program to gain the support of the OAs.

DoT believes that it is necessary to broaden traditional notions of development to multiple learning strategies, both individual and organizational, that might rely on many approaches besides courses. These might include job rotation, job shadowing, mentoring, or coaching. Supervisors and managers need to have learning strategies as part of their training, and human resources professionals should serve as consultants to managers and supervisors in these matters.

The top-level DoT management deals with turnover by requiring that current and future leaders be identified. Mid-level DoT employees—the "careerists" and the future successors of top managers—are brought in whenever key decisions and plans are being made. This means that mid-level employees feel involved in and "own" top-level decisions. Also, all levels of management are included in leadership conferences in different agencies.

A major concern at DoT has been linking learning activities with workforce changes and the necessary transfer of human capital. To attract high-quality employees, DoT agencies must demonstrate the ability to support their continued learning and development. The L&D program thinks of this as the Arthur Andersen model—an employee could go anywhere after working there because it is well known that Arthur Andersen invests heavily in employee learning. It is also important to attend to professional sense of fulfillment and quality of work life as well as related issues in employee recruitment and retention.

DoT has endeavored to link workforce planning and training by looking at how current competencies meet needs, and if they do not, how to bridge that gap. They have employed performance consultants to help develop competency modules and they hope to use the L&D framework as a tool to fill in the gaps.

Evaluation of Organizational Performance

Each overall agency strategic goal has a list of performance indicators that are used to assess progress. The goals outlined in the annual performance plan will be used to judge improvement and will be communicated to Congress in annual performance reports. The plans will link the ten OAs in the department and the 140 budgeted program activities with the strategic goals (DoT, 1997, p. 40).

After concluding a study assessing the department's program evaluation practices, a comprehensive five-year program evaluation plan has been adopted in collaboration with the subagencies. The department will conduct evaluations of major programs as they relate to strategic goals through program offices of the subagencies. (For example, highway cost allocation, which is linked to the economic growth and trade strategic goal will be studied through the Federal Highway Administration.)

Three main sources of data will serve as indicators of performance for the department: outcome data from statistical sources, external reviews and program evaluation, and customer surveys and evaluation of customer standards (DoT, 1997, p. 43). Examples of statistical sources include the National Transportation Statistics, National Transit Database, National Bridge Inventory, and Hazardous Material Information System. There is, however, no central system for reporting or tracking learning and development activities, although the Human Resources Department is trying to develop a "human resources information system," which would include this information linked with other relevant data. All training officers of the separate

OAs are required to keep records, but every agency has its own record-keeping system. L&D rarely has occasion to use these data. Every few years, the idea of developing a broad human resources information system surfaces, but the system has not yet been built.

FEDERAL HIGHWAY ADMINISTRATION

Background

The Intelligent Transportation System (ITS) program in the FHWA uses technology to better operate and manage existing transportation systems (e.g., providing better information for travelers).

The current DoT workforce is not adequate to deal with the emerging transportation-relevant technology. A large part of the problem is competition for technology workers with other federal agencies and with the private sector. The FHWA representative emphasized that public agencies must find new approaches in human resource management to recruit and retain a qualified workforce. The surface transportation and transit programs have been behind others in the public sector in changing the way they do business (e.g., deregulation and privatization). Human resource development professionals are concerned that this area of the transportation sector will not be able to make the kinds of changes that are required to hire and train a competitive workforce. Many of the transportation programs are currently heavily reliant on "pork barrels" (earmarked government funds for their programs and projects) that do not reward excellence.

The K–12 pipeline is not providing what is needed for the future entry-level transportation workforce, and thus the skill pool is shrinking. Even at higher levels, problems exist. Transportation has traditionally relied on workers with civil engineering training, which is no longer attracting enough undergraduate majors in universities. Further, the transportation professionals of the future will need a breadth of knowledge from other disciplines (economics, political science, etc.) as well as depth in their own field.

FHWA has concluded that "the new transportation professional of the future has to be systematically envisioned" as a starting point. Most of the politicians and appointees involved with transportation policy and programming understand these issues (and the necessity of learning and development), but few know how to make the needed improvement happen.

Development of the Strategic Plan

From the perspective of a professional development consultant hired by FHWA, a comprehensive, broad-based, and targeted approach to learning and development was missing from FHWA. In setting out to develop a strategic plan, the consultant identified professional capacity building (PCB) for an intelligent transportation system as an appropriate starting point for improving education and development activities in the department. Creating a focus was critical to getting started; he noted "you have to create change in bite-sized chunks."

The FHWA consultant was not sure what would be appropriate at the beginning of his DoT tenure. However, after the initial phase of being immersed in the department's bureaucratic politics, he developed a plan to conduct awareness seminars to highlight the overall need for change within the FHWA and the need for the PCB program. Because of his relatively small budget, he sought, from the beginning, to keep the program small and to focus it on higher-level professionals. The development of the successful strategic plan and its implementation were based largely on the skills and experience of the consultant—both how to approach it and what to teach (the content).

The awareness seminars were designed to highlight the need for professional development by addressing the issue of why the FHWA should be doing business differently, as well as raising questions such as how to get institutions within FHWA to work together in this effort.

The awareness seminars initially encountered substantial resistance. After a period of uncertainty, a strategic plan was gradually pulled together. FHWA is interested in creating partnerships with other institutions for the development and provision of their education and training activities but currently lacks the technical infrastructure and people to support it. Bureaucratic turf is a major issue that makes partnerships a serious challenge. It has been hard to develop academic partnerships (e.g., between the National Highway Institute and colleges or junior colleges), but continuing education is becoming a big business for public universities, and distance learning carries a lot of the weight for continuing education courses. Therefore, the web-based courses developed under the ITS-PCB initiative could become moneymakers for some schools.

The Office of the Secretary for Transportation Human Resource Department is not considered important for FHWA's PCB program because the resources it provides are too generic to be applicable. But the One DoT effort could help cut across barriers and make partnerships between OAs. Secretary Slater has gone as far as anyone could go with this, but the effort is limited by stovepiped and regional political concerns. A few other visionary people in DoT will also push the comprehensive learning agenda, however.

What is missing in DoT is a link between professional education and compensation—an enormous omission for an agency that wants to be a "learning organization." It is critical to link financial incentives to intellectual motivation to create real learning organizations. Courses should be tied to jobs and career paths, and learners should be rewarded. If an agency cannot do that, it will be unable to attract or keep good people.

Discussion

The Department of Transportation as a whole, and FHWA in particular, offer important lessons for the Chancellor's office on issues related to the development of its vision and strategic plan. The FHWA consultant recommends that the Chancellor's office find an initial focus, just as the consultant did with professional capacity building for the future of intelligent transportation. It should then map the playing field to clearly identify the customers and other stakeholders, characterize what is happening in their environment, and understand what the ET&D providers in its domain are contributing. After this initial analysis, the Chancellor's office should work toward establishing a standard and creating a model for ET&D. Finally, it should diffuse the importance of learning throughout the customer terrain.

BIBLIOGRAPHY

Armey, R., L. Craig, D. Burton, B. Livingston, and J. Kasich, *The Results Act: It's the Law*, 1997, available at http://freedom.house.gov/results/finalreport/rfin1.asp.

Association of American Universities, Committee on Graduate Education, http://www.tulane.edu/~aau/GradEdRpt.html.

Baldwin, J. A., "Blueprint for the Chancellor for Education and Professional Development," memorandum for the Deputy Secretary of Defense, September 15, 1998.

Bank of Montreal, http://www.traininguniversity.com/magazine/may_jun99/feature1.html.

Beinhocker, E. D., "Robust Adaptive Strategies," *Sloan Management Review*, Vol. 40, No. 3, 1999, pp. 95–106.

Bensimon, E. M., and A. Neuman, *Redesigning Collegiate Leadership: Teams and Teamwork in Higher Education*, Johns Hopkins University Press, Baltimore, Maryland, 1993.

Birnbaum, R., *How Colleges Work: The Cybernetics of Academic Organization and Leadership*, Jossey-Bass, San Francisco, California, 1988.

Board of Regents, University System of Georgia Comprehensive Plan 1996–97, presented by the Strategic Planning Committee of the Board of Regents, Donald Leebern, Chair, to the Board of Regents, July 9, 1997, Board of Regents, University System of Georgia, avail-

able at http://www.peachnet.edu/admin/planning/compplan.
html.

Builder, C. H., and J. A. Dewar, "A Time for Planning? If Not Now,
When?" *Parameters,* Vol. 24, No. 2, 1994, pp. 4–16.

California Higher Education Policy Center, *A Promise Worth Keeping,*
San Jose, California, 1997, available at http://www.policycenter.
org/ct_0597/cts_0597.html.

California State Board of Education, *Comprehensive Vision, Mission,
and Goals Statement,* available at http://www.cde.ca.gov/board/
vmgoal.html.

California State University, *The Cornerstones Report V,* 1997,
available at http://www.calstate.edu/cornerstones/reports/
cornerstones_report/index.html.

California State University, *Cornerstones Implementation Plan, 1998,*
available at http://www.calstate.edu/cornerstones/reports/
implment.html.

Christensen, Clayton M., *The Innovator's Dilemma,* Harvard Business
School Press, Boston, Massachusetts, 1997.

Clementi, A. J., *Report of the Council on Long Range Planning and
Development,* American Medical Association, 1998, available
at http://www.ama-assn.org/meetings/public/annual98/reports/
clrpd/clrpd03.htm .

Clinton, W. J., *Blair House Papers,* Government Printing Office,
Washington, D.C., 1997.

Clugston, R.M.J., *Strategic Adaptation in an Organized Anarchy:
Priority Setting and Resource Allocation in the Liberal Arts College
of a Public Research University,* University of Minnesota, Min-
neapolis, Minnesota, 1987.

Cohen, William, Defense Reform Initiative Directive 41 study,
*Blueprint for the Chancellor for Education and Professional
Development,* September 1998.

Collins, James C., and Jerry I. Porras, *Built to Last: Successful Habits
of Visionary Companies,* HarperCollins, 1994.

Collis, David, *When Industries Change Revisited: New Scenarios for Higher Education,* paper presented at the Forum for the Future of Higher Education, Aspen Institute, September 26–28, 1999, available at http://emcc.mit.edu/forum/pdf/futures00/industrieschange.pdf.

Commission of the States, *1997 State Postsecondary Education Structures Sourcebook: State Coordinating and Governing Boards.* Education Commission of the States, Denver, Colorado, 1997.

Committee on Governmental Affairs, United States Senate, *Government Performance and Results Act of 1993 Report,* 1993, available at http://server.conginst.org/conginst/results/gprarpt.html.

Creating Your Corporate University, http://www.woohoou.com/corporat.htm.

Defense Manpower Data Center, *Forces Readiness and Manpower Information System,* 1999, available at http://www.dmdc.osd.mil/formis/owa/FORMIS.AA_GO.

Defense Manpower Data Center, *1995–2000 Analysis of End Strength and Demographic Trends Among DoD Civilians,* Washington, D.C., 2001.

Department of the Army, *The Army Vision: Soldiers On Point for the Nation . . . Persuasive in Peace, Invincible in War,* 2000, available at http://www.army.mil/armyvision/vision.htm.

Department of the Army, *Army Training,* AR-350-1, Washington, D.C.

Department of the Army, *Management of Army Individual Training Requirements,* AR-350-10, Washington, D.C.

Department of the Army, *Training Device Policies and Management,* AR-350-38, Washington, D.C.

Department of the Army, *Training in Units,* AR-351-41, Washington, D.C.

Department of the Army, *Individual Military Education and Training,* AR-351-1, Washington, D.C.

Department of the Army, Training and Doctrine Command, *Training the Force*, FM 25-100, Washington, D.C.

Department of the Army, Training and Doctrine Command, *Battle-Focused Training*, FM 25-101, Washington, D.C.

Department of Defense, *Report on the Bottom-Up Review*, Washington, D.C., October 1993.

Department of Defense, *Quadrennial Defense Review*, Washington, D.C., May 1997.

Department of Education, *Strategic Plan*, available at http://www.ed.gov/pubs/StratPln/.

Department of Labor, *Futurework: Trends and Challenges for Work in the 21st Century*, U.S. Government Printing Office, Washington, D.C., 1999.

Department of Transportation, *Corporate Management Strategy Flagships*, 1999, available at http://www.dot.gov/onedot/newctl.htm.

Department of Transportation, *Strategic Plan*, 1997, available at http://www.dot.gov/hot/dotplan.html.

Dewar, J., C. H. Builder, W. M. Hix, and M. H. Levin, *Assumption-Based Planning: A Planning Tool for Very Uncertain Times*, RAND, MR-114-A, Santa Monica, California, 1993.

Dill, David, "Designing Academic Audit: Lessons Learned in Europe and Asia," *Quality in Higher Education*, Vol. 6, No. 3, 2000, pp. 187–207.

Evans, Philip, and Thomas S. Wurster, *Blown to Bits: How the New Economics of Information Transforms Strategy*, Harvard Business School Press, Boston, Massachusetts, 1999.

Ewell, P. T., "The Current Pattern of State-Level Assessment: Results of a National Inventory," *Assessment Update*, Vol. 8, No. 3, 1996, pp. 1–15.

Ewell, P. T., "Identifying Indicators of Curricular Quality," in G. Gaff and J. Ratcliff (eds.), *Handbook of the Undergraduate Curriculum*, Jossey-Bass Inc., San Francisco, California, 1997.

Ewell, P. T., "Accountability and Assessment in a Second Decade: New Looks or Same Old Story?" *Assessing Impact: Evidence and Action*, Presentations from the 1997 American Association for Higher Education Conference on Assessment and Quality, American Association for Higher Education, Washington, D.C., 1997.

Ewell, P. T., *A Delicate Balance: The Role of Evaluation in Management*, National Center for Higher Education Management Systems, Boulder, Colorado, 1999.

Ewell, P.T., *Examining a Brave New World: How Accreditation Might Be Different*, Council on Higher Education Accreditation, Washington, D.C., 1999.

Gates, Susan M., Catherine H. Augustine, Roger Benjamin, Tora K. Bikson, Eric Derghazarian, Tessa Kaganoff, Dina G. Levy, Joy S. Moini, and Ron W. Zimmer, *Ensuring the Quality and Productivity of Education and Professional Development Activities: A Review of Approaches and Lessons for DoD*, RAND, MR-1257-OSD, 2001.

Gill, Brian P., *The Governance of the City University of New York: A System at Odds with Itself*, RAND, MR-1141-EDU, Santa Monica, California, 2000.

General Accounting Office, *Executive Guide: Effectively Implementing the Government Performance and Results Act*, GAO/GGD-96-118, Washington, D.C., 1996.

General Accounting Office, *The Government Performance and Results Act: 1997 Governmentwide Implementation Will Be Uneven*, GAO/GGD-97-109, Washington, D.C., June 1997a.

General Accounting Office, *The Results Act: Observations on the Social Security Administration's June 1997 Draft Strategic Plan*, GAO/HEHS-97-179R, Washington, D.C., July 1997b.

General Accounting Office, *Managing for Results: Critical Issues for Improving Federal Agencies' Strategic Plans*, GAO/GGD-97-180, Washington, D.C., September 1997c.

General Accounting Office, *The Results Act: Observations on the Department of Defense's Draft Strategic Plan*, GAO/NSIAD-97-219R, Washington, D.C., 1997d.

General Accounting Office, *Agencies' Strategic Plans Under GPRA: Key Questions to Facilitate Congressional Review*, GAO/GGD-10.1.16, Washington, D.C., 1997e.

General Accounting Office, *Observations on the Department of Defense's Annual Performance Plan*, GAO/NSIAD-99-188R, Washington, D.C., 1998.

General Accounting Office, *Observations on the Department of Defense's Performance Plan for Fiscal Year 2000*, GAO/NSIAD-99-178R, Washington, D.C., 1999a.

General Accounting Office, *Agency Performance Plans: Examples of Practices That Can Improve Usefulness to Decisionmakers*, GAO/GGD-AIMD-99-69, Washington, D.C., 1999b.

Gibbs, M., "Pay Competitiveness and Quality of Civil Service Scientist and Engineers in DoD Laboratories," RAND, unpublished.

Glidden, R., *The Contemporary Context of Accreditation: Challenges in a Changing Environment*, keynote address for 2nd CHEA "Usefulness" Conference, Washington, D.C., 1998, available at http://www.chea.org/Events/Usefulness/98May/9805Glidden.html.

Government Performance and Results Act of 1993, 31 U.S.C. 1101.

Haine, S. F., "Measuring the Mission: Using a Scorecard Approach in Not-For-Profit Organizations," *Journal of Strategic Performance Measurement*, Vol. 3, No. 2, 1999, pp. 13–19.

Hamel, Gary, and C. K. Prahalad, *Competing for the Future*, Harvard Business School Press, Boston, Massachusetts, 1994.

Harvard Business School Press, *Harvard Business Review on Managing Uncertainty*, 1999.

Heracleous, L., "Strategic Thinking or Strategic Planning," *Long Range Planning*, Vol. 31, No. 3, 1998, pp. 481–487.

Human Resources Development Council, *Getting Results Through Learning*, Washington, D.C., June 1997.

Joint Chiefs of Staff, *Joint Vision 2010*, Department of Defense, 1997, available at http://www.dtic.mil/jv2020/history.htm.

Joint Chiefs of Staff, *Joint Vision 2020*, Department of Defense, May 2000, available at http://www.dtic.mil/jv2020.pdf.

Joint Staff for the Committee, *A Study of the Need for Additional Centers of Public Higher Education in California*, California State Department of Education, Sacramento, California, 1957.

Joint Vision Implementation Master Plan, 1998, available at http://www.dtic.mil/doctrine/jel/ccsd/cjcsi/3010_02.pdf.

Kaplan, R. S., and D. P. Norton, "Using the Balanced Scorecard as a Strategic Management System," *Harvard Business Review*, Vol. 74, No. 1, 1996, pp. 75–85.

Kentucky Council for Postsecondary Education, *2020 Vision: An Agenda for Kentucky's System of Higher Education*, Lexington, Kentucky, 1998.

Kerr, Clark, *Preserving the Master Plan*, The California Higher Education Policy Center, San Jose, California, 1994.

Lee, J. B., and S. B. Clery, *Employer Aid for Postsecondary Education*, Department of Education, National Center for Education Statistics, Washington, D.C., June 1999.

Levy, D. G., H. J. Thie, A. A. Robbert, S. Naftel, C. Cannon, R. Ehrenberg, and M. Gershwin, *Characterizing the Future Defense Workforce*, RAND, MR-1304-OSD, 2001.

Locke, Christopher (ed.), *The Cluetrain Manifesto: The End of Business As Usual*, Perseus Books, Boulder, Colorado, 2000.

Malcolm Baldrige Quality Award Program, *Education Criteria for Performance Excellence*, 1999, available at http://www.quality.nist.gov.

Markides, C. C., "A Dynamic View of Strategy," *Sloan Management Review*, Vol. 40, No. 3, 1999, pp. 55–63.

Master Plan Survey Team, *A Master Plan for Higher Education in California 1960–1975*, California State Department of Education, Sacramento, California, 1960.

McGee, G. E., *American Medical Association Strategic Planning Process: Report of the Council on Long Range Planning and Development*, American Medical Association, 1999.

Meister, J. C., *Corporate Universities: Lessons in Building a World-Class Work Force*, McGraw-Hill, New York, 1998.

Mihm, Christopher J., *Managing for Results: Observations on Agencies' Strategic Plans*, General Accounting Office, GAO/T-GGD-98-66, Washington, D.C., 1998.

Mintzberg, Henry, *The Rise and Fall of Strategic Planning*, The Free Press, New York, 1994.

Mintzberg, H., and J. Lampel, "Reflecting on the Strategy Process," *Sloan Management Review*, Spring 1999, pp. 21–30.

Mintzberg, H., B. Ahlstand, and J. Lampel, *Strategy Safari: A Guided Tour Through the Wilds of Strategic Management*, The Free Press, New York, 1998.

Modahl, Mary, *Now or Never: How Companies Must Change Today to Win the Battle for Internet Consumers*, HarperBusiness, New York, 1999.

Nelson, A. M., *Final Report of the Ad Hoc Committee on Structure, Governance, and Operations*, American Medical Association, 1998, available at http://www.ama-assn.org/meetings/public/interim1999/reports/onsite/rtf/bot19.rtf.

Office of the Assistant Secretary of Defense for Force Management Policy, *Management Reform Memorandum 3: Streamlining the Management of Educational and Professional Development Programs*, December 1997.

Office of Management and Budget, *Performance of Commercial Activities*, Circular No. A-76 (Revised), Washington, D.C., August 4, 1983.

Office of Management and Budget, *Preparation and Submission of Strategic Plans and Annual Performance Plans*, Circular No. A-11, Part 2, 1998.

Porter, Michael E., *Competitive Strategy: Techniques for Analyzing Industries and Competitors*, Free Press, New York, 1998.

Quality Assurance Agency (United Kingdom), http://www.qaa.ac.uk/.

Ruppert, S. S., "Roots and Realities of State-Level Performance Indicator Systems," *New Directions for Higher Education: Assessing Performance in an Age of Accountability: Case Studies, XXIII, No. 3*, Number 91, Fall 1995, pp. 11–23.

Schwartz, P., *Art of the Long View*, Doubleday/Currency, New York, 1991.

Select Committee on the Master Plan, *The California Master Plan for Higher Education in the Seventies and Beyond*, Report and Recommendations of the Select Committee on the Master Plan for Higher Education to the Coordinating Council for Higher Education, Council Report 72-6, November 1972.

Setear, J., C. H. Builder, M. D. Baccus, and W. Madewell, *The Army in a Changing World: The Role of Organizational Vision*, RAND, R-3882-A, 1990.

Simpson, D. G., "Why Most Strategic Planning Is a Waste of Time and What You Can Do About It,"*Long Range Planning*, Vol. 31, No. 3, 1998, pp.476–480.

Smoak Jr., R. D., *American Medical Association Vision and Strategic Directions: Report of the Board of Trustees*, 1999.

Social Security Administration, http://www.ssa.gov.

Social Security Administration, *Strategic Plan*, 1997, available at http://www.ssa.gov/asp/index.html.

Steers, R. M., L. W. Porter, and G. A. Bigley, *Motivation and Leadership at Work*, sixth edition, McGraw-Hill, New York, 1996.

Szutz, J., "Higher Education Systems and Strategic Planning," in G. Gaither (ed.), *The Multicampus System Perspectives on Practice and Prospects*, Stylus Publishers, Sterling, Virginia, 1999.

Technical Committee on Costs of Higher Education in California, *A Report on the Costs of Higher Education in California 1960–1975*, prepared for the Master Plan Survey Team, the Liaison Committee of the Regents of the University of California, and the State Board of Education, Berkeley and Sacramento, January 1960.

Technical Committee on Institutional Capacities and Area Needs, *Institutional Capacities and Area Needs of California Public Higher Education 1960–1975*, prepared for the Liaison Committee of the Regents of the University of California, the State Board of Education, and the Master Plan Survey Team, Berkeley and Sacramento, February 1961.

Tennessee Valley Authority University, http://www. traininguniversity.com/magazine/may-jun99/feature4.html..

Texas Higher Education Coordinating Board, http://www.thecb. state.tx.us/.

Tierney, W. G., *The Responsive University*, Johns Hopkins University Press, Baltimore, Maryland, 1997.

Tierney, W. G., *Restructuring Postsecondary Education: Problems and Possibilities*, Johns Hopkins University Press, Baltimore, Maryland, 1999.

21st Century Challenges and Desired Operational Capabilities, 1997, available at http://www.dtic.mil/jcs/ (Joint Vision Historical Documents).

The University System of Georgia's Vision Statement, *Access to Academic Excellence for the New Millennium: A Vision for the University System of Georgia*, n.d., available at http://www.peachnet. edu/pubs/annual_rep/1998/vision.html.

Urban Universities Portfolio Project: Assuring Quality for Multiple Publics, available at http://www.imir.iupui.edu/portfolio/.

Vaill, Peter B., "The Purposing of High-Performing Systems," *Organizational Dynamics*, Autumn 1982.

Western Association of Schools and Colleges, *An Invitation to Dialogue*, Alameda, California, 1998, available at www.wascweb.org.

Western Association of Schools and Colleges, *Invitation to Dialogue II: Proposed Framework for a New Model of Accreditation*, Alameda, California, 1999, available at www.wascweb.org.